Head to House

How to run your house effectively

edited by

Vivian Anthony and Charles Bush

John Catt Educational Limited

Head to House
First Published 2000

by John Catt Educational Ltd,
Great Glemham, Saxmundham, Suffolk IP17 2DH
Tel: 01728 663666 Fax: 01728 663415
E-mail: enquiries@johncatt.co.uk
Website: www.johncatt.com

ISBN: 0 901577 54 5

Set and designed by
John Catt Educational Limited

Printed and bound in Great Britain by Unwin Brothers, The Gresham Press, Old Woking, Surrey GU22 9LH, England

Foreword

Esther Rantzen

When my children were toddlers, I did not for a moment anticipate that I would send any of them to boarding school. I had been responsible, with the ChildLine team and the staff of the television programme, "That's Life!", for exposing a boarding school which was owned by a paedophile. It is closed now, and he served a prison sentence. But that experience meant I was more aware than many parents of the potential dangers of sending a child away from home to be educated. I also knew from the boys themselves how difficult they had found it to confide in their parents, who had sacrificed so much to give them what they hoped was a good education. Why then did I send my own son away to school at fourteen?

The first and most important reason was that our son wanted to go. I was interested to read in the essays contained in this excellent and informative book that is true of more than ninety per cent of boarding school pupils. They are there from choice. Not all children would opt for a gregarious, community life. I have an introverted daughter for whom it would have been unsuitable. But our son chose boarding school and thrived there.

The second reason is that adolescents are a species on their own. They look different from their parents, they sound different, they are often nocturnal, they indulge in odd and incomprehensible rituals, and they scorn the company of any family members more than twenty years older than they are. I was, to be frank, unsure that I was the best influence on my teenage son, or indeed that I had any influence at all. I welcomed the training, skill and talent of the houseparents and teachers at his school. They seemed to understand these years far better than I did. On a holiday in Kenya, I once visited a Masai village inhabited only by sixteen year old warriors. As part of their manhood rituals they left their homes and created the village together, where they learned to hunt lions, and danced snake dances, and covered themselves with dung and ochre. So I was well prepared for our son to do much the same, at about the same time in his life.

He tells me that it was quite tough for him as a new boy at school, although he never confessed it at the time. But he also says that once he had settled in, he was extremely happy there, and believes he has been given opportunities and challenges which he found exciting and worthwhile. He and his friends have matured into strong, kind young men, and although I feel proud of him and them, I know that I cannot really claim any credit. Much of their maturity is due to the life-style and education they have enjoyed at boarding school.

There are huge pressures on young people these days, as I know from the thousands of calls made to ChildLine. Exams, league tables, sex, drugs, rock and roll and all the other demands of work and play can make them depressed, lonely, exhausted, and fearful. At the same time, they can be resilient, humorous and compassionate. Boarding school teachers deal, day and night, with these contradictions. Reading the testimony of those who have contributed to this book leaves me breathless with admiration, not least for the teachers' stamina. And although my experience in child protection leads me to believe that children living away from home need the protection of a confidential phone-line, just in case things go badly wrong, the most heart-warming aspect of this book is the love and understanding of children which pervades every chapter, and for which, as a mother of a boarding school pupil, I have every reason to be extremely grateful.

Contents

Contents

The photographs throughout are by John Keeling, except for that on page 59, which is by Rupert Watts.

Editors' note

There is a fund of good advice to be found in this series of chapters and we are grateful to Heads who have given time to contribute their wisdom as well as their light-hearted reminiscences. It is clear that no one remains unaffected by the experience of living in a boarding House and just as the lives of children who experience the delight of full boarding are wholly changed, so too are those who are entrusted with the responsibility of care. The 'total community' of the boarding environment causes great richness and diversity of experience.

We make no apology for the universal use of the term 'Houseparent' as the thoroughly modern and politically correct term representing the person most of us know as a Housemaster or Housemistress or HM or HsM. We are aware that some schools promote the term 'Houseparents' as relating to a couple who run a House together, but in the singular sense, within this book, this is not our meaning. Houseparent is used throughout as a gender-insensitive term. It may make the text a little stilted in some places but in our new predominantly co-educational world we hope it will help us to look to the future with the best in good boarding practice.

Charles Bush and Vivian Anthony, Joint Editors

Introduction

by James Sabben-Clare

Headmaster, Winchester College
Chairman of HMC 1999

An historical perspective

"In each of the lower Chambers let there be at least two scholars of good behaviour, more advanced than the other scholars in maturity, sense and knowledge, who are to superintend the studies of their other chamber-companions and supervise them diligently, and when required, bring true report and information about their behaviour and conduct and the progress of their studies to the Warden, Vice-Warden and Master from time to time."

This excerpt from William of Wykeham's Statutes for Winchester College, written in 1400, appears to be the earliest reference to the responsibilities that might arise from the provision of boarding education. Wykeham was in this, as in so many other things, an innovator. Thomas Arnold is sometimes thought of as the inventor of the prefectorial system; in fact, however, Arnold's reforms at Rugby had been foreshadowed more than four centuries before. What they both had in common was a primary reliance on older pupils rather than on adults to look after the day to day behaviour and activities of the younger ones. The concept of a Housemaster, Housemistress or Houseparent in any terms that we would recognise today took a very long time to develop. This is surprising in view of the deeply rooted tradition of boarding education in this country.

The young boys who presented themselves for election as scholars of Winchester were not to be limited to those who lived locally. In fact the Statutes stipulated that preference would be given to those who came from the counties within the see of Winchester, a much more extensive area than it is today, covering the counties from Dorset to Kent, from Sussex to Oxfordshire. Some lived even further away still. Consequently there had to be facilities provided for them to sleep and eat, take exercise (not much) and receive medical care (even less), as well as work and worship. To provide some sort of substitute for parental care at home Wykeham lodged his scholars in Chambers on the ground floor of the main courtyard. Each Chamber contained about twelve boys, with a mix of ages so that an element of familial structure was maintained. That same system still operates in College at Winchester, over 600 years later.

Mobile telephones, e-mail and faxes not withstanding, the mail is still much awaited.

There was of course plenty of adult influence in the lives of these young people, but for the most part it would have been quite remote and formal; mostly a matter of taking the lessons, checking for absence and other breaches of the Statutes, and applying discipline accordingly. Feminine influence there was none. Indeed women were to be rigorously excluded. Wykeham's Statutes expressly forbade any female servants to enter the College precincts 'unless they be of such age and appearance as to excite no suspicion'.

What the boys got up to when they had time of their own was a matter for them alone. There were only two masters, and although they could, if so minded, have done some 'Housemastering' when there were only the original 70 scholars to look after, the early addition of extra pupils made this progressively less possible.

These outside pupils, the first fee-payers, either lodged with one of the masters or else, as happened at Shrewsbury when it was founded in 1552, lived in the town and just came in to lessons. There was no conception of boarding as a valuable educational experience in its own right, or as an opportunity to learn about independence and responsibility. It was simply the only means of getting access to schools of established quality if there was none in your own town. Nor was there any suggestion that the master was in *loco parentis*.

Indeed Richard Mulcaster, who at this time wrote the first systematic survey of schools and schooling in the country, suggested that the two roles could not realistically be combined. In 1581 he wrote: 'Methinks it is enough for the master to take upon him the training alone. If parents dwell not near the school, let some neighbours be hosts and deliver the master of the parents' care; for they be distinct offices, to be a parent and a master'.

The situation began to change towards the end of the following century, when it became an increasingly common practice for the nobility to send their children away to board at school rather than keeping them at home with their own tutor. No doubt the presence of such sprigs of the aristocracy in certain schools attracted other socially ambitious parents to do likewise. The numbers at Eton grew through the first half of the 18th century, reaching a peak of 522 in 1765. Most of them would have lived in the town (hence the name of Oppidans) under the not very vigilant eye of a Dominie or Dame.

At the same time encouragement to take boarding pupils came from a very different quarter. Towns of any size would by this date expect to have at least one endowed Grammar School. The statutes that controlled these schools would, among other details, stipulate what the stipend of the master was to be, and the governing boards would be sure to see that the statutory limit was not exceeded. As decades and even centuries passed, the only way that the master could earn a proper living for himself was to take on extra pupils from outside the locality. They would live under his care and, more importantly, pay their fees direct to him.

This still did not prevent the sort of criticism voiced by John Clarke, Headmaster of Hull School, in an essay on Grammar School education (1730). He said that most such schools were 'little more than houses of correction for the boys of the neighbourhood', and as for the larger city schools, a boy would find himself 'in a promiscuous, numerous herd of rude, wild boys, many of them very vicious, where if he escapes without the loss of his innocence or without a strong infection from the foulest of vices, it must be next to a miracle'.

It was the Nonconformist parents who decided that they wished to have schools which would not only protect their children from such contamination but also bring them to a proper understanding of good and disciplined behaviour. The Moravian Brothers at Fulneck, the Quakers at Ackworth, and the Methodists at Kingswood sought to meet these needs by creating schools where boarding was an essential part of the programme of moral instruction and not just a matter of practical convenience or financial advantage. The discipline was, however, fearsome. At Kingswood the day began at 4am with an hour's prayer and private reading and continued in the same vein until bedtime at 8pm There was no time allowed for play, and parents were kept well away.

Such examples of pastoral supervision were too extreme for most, and at the great national schools conditions got no better for the pupils until the middle of the 19th century. They were understaffed, and the baneful hand of tradition discouraged masters from interfering in the every day lives of the pupils. As a result violence and anarchy ruled, the only control being exercised on the whim of senior boys. There were Housemasters of a kind such that at Eton, for instance, the more aristocratic pupils would lodge with masters rather than Dames; but their obligations did not amount to much more than calling names over at the specified times of day. Pastoral care was an optional extra.

Though a surprising number seemed to have enjoyed this bruising experience, the graphic tales of bullying, cruelty and intimidation enshrined in the literature of the period have cast a long shadow over our schools. No doubt there are still people in the world whose idea of Public School life owes more to *Tom Brown's Schooldays* than to any number of current prospectuses and ISIS publications. Back in the unreformed days, the truth was sometimes even worse than the fiction.

At Eton on 2 March 1825 two boys were persuaded to settle a trivial dispute in the time-honoured way by fighting it out on the playing field. After more than two hours both boys were at a standstill. The younger one, Francis Ashley, a son of

Lord Shaftesbury, collapsed and never regained consciousness. The Housemaster was neither informed at the time nor later held responsible.

Credit for changing this bestial culture is usually ascribed to Edward Thring. When he took over as Headmaster of Uppingham in 1853, he needed to expand the numbers in the school from the parlous figure of 23 which he inherited. But he was equally determined to avoid the large open plan dormitories and school rooms which led to so many abuses. He therefore invited a number of young men onto his staff with the capital to build boarding houses of their own, stipulating that none was to contain more than 30 boys; for this, he felt, was the most that any man could properly look after. The boys were all to have studies of their own to work in, and separate cubicles at night.

This became the pattern at other schools. At Winchester the first boarding House was opened in 1859 and two others quickly followed. The reasons were ones of health and hygiene as much as anything else; the sanitation of the main Commoners building was so poor that infection was frequent and death from typhoid sadly not unknown. A new Headmaster, George Ridding, arriving in 1867 decided that no more boys were to be lodged centrally and all were to go into boarding Houses.

As at Uppingham, these Winchester houses were built with private capital, and the Housemasters concerned had to recoup their costs by the profit they could make from the fee-paying pupils. This could well have compromised the level of care and standard of accommodation they offered, and it was not long before the Governing Body of the College bought the Houses from them. Even then, the domestic management was entirely in the hands of the individual. The House was being run as a hotel and, put crudely, a Housemaster who kept his boys cold and hungry would make more money out of them than one who treated them more generously. On the other hand there were plenty of instances of Housemasters with private incomes using their own money to enhance the lives of their pupils. This 'hotel' system continued to operate at Winchester until the Second War, and at some other schools later still.

Once the idea was established of placing pupils in manageable groups under the dedicated care of an adult, the House became increasingly the focus of all boarding school life. Loyalty to the House was often stronger than that to the school, and the relationship between Houseparent and pupil could develop into life-long friendship. A real sense of family community was thus established, with the Houseparents, matron, and tutors having essential parts to play in it.

So long as there was also an effective prefectorial structure which looked after the day to day administration and discipline, the role of the Houseparent was essentially paternalistic, and as distant or as close as the individual felt inclined. In the 1960s there was a change when the traditional hierarchies were loosened. They had long been sustained by the elaborate balancing of petty privileges and responsibilities; but a new radically minded generation was not interested in the former and often less committed to the latter. A greater burden therefore fell directly on the adults in charge of them.

In the last thirty years this burden has continued to increase. Many factors have combined to the same end: the economic pressure to raise the number of pupils in a House, intrusive legislation and bureaucracy, demanding and potentially litigious parents, ever higher expectations in terms of comforts and facilities, the materialism of youth culture, the mobile 'phone, open access to the Internet, and so on.

Running a House these days requires great resilience of body and spirit. It is not for the self-indulgent or the fainthearted. But the rewards, in terms of personal and professional fulfilment, for such close involvement with the development of young people, are as great as ever, and for many mark a satisfying culmination to their teaching career. Besides, there is a far greater recognition now of the need for careful training, induction and continuous support. This volume itself bears witness to that.

James Sabben-Clare was a boarder and later Master in College at Winchester; since 1985 he has been Headmaster. He was Chairman of HMC in 1999.

Chapter 1

The First Few Weeks

by Nick England

Headmaster, Ryde School

Dear Robert

How kind of you to write and let me know that you will be moving into School House next Autumn Term. What splendid news, many congratulations! I am very pleased that your skills in the classroom, as a hockey coach and, most recently, as Head of Economics have been recognised. I am sure that you have now got the experience, judgement and wisdom to make a success of the next stage.

You asked me if I would put down a few thoughts to help you on the way. I am happy to do this, and what follows is quite a personal account. You have to run your own House, and you will have to develop your own philosophy and style; finding out what others do is a good way to begin.

There is absolutely no doubt that you are about to start the most important job in education. If you run School House for ten years, you will see about 150 boys through the most formative years of their lives. You will have a far greater influence than any of their classroom teachers, the Head, or the Chief Inspector of Schools. You will leave an indelible imprint on their minds; they will remember your enthusiasms and your values forever, as well as the help, guidance and encouragement you offer them. They will remember with gratitude how you saw them through a bad spell. I have heard it said that a large school can survive a bad Head for several years, but a bad Houseparent can turn a House bad within weeks. This is why you face the most demanding of jobs, which will test your leadership skills, courage and stamina to the limit.

I hope that you will go on a course for prospective Houseparents in the next few months. It is most helpful to be able to discuss scenarios you may face, and to make friends with other people in your position. However, nothing will prepare you for the first week in office. I have had several shocks in my life; my first week at a boarding school aged seven; my first week at university, when I realised that the level of difficulty of the work had just taken a quantum leap; my first week as Head, facing hundreds of new faces, all of whom knew who I was, and I knowing nothing of them; but it was the first week as a Houseparent which was the most hectic of experiences.

Moving house and changing jobs are two of life's most stressful events; you will do both of these when you move into School House. I know you will only move three hundred yards, and you will still be teaching Economics, but your life will change. When we moved into Challoner's we were just about organised by the beginning of term; we had done some decorating, fixed up curtain poles, and Sue was busy sewing the hems of curtains. I had made sure the boys' side of the House was in good order, sorted out the keys, pinned up notices of House rules, House routine and ruled neat lines in the pocket money book although I hope you will run your house account by computer. I had spent happy hours, clearing out files, and learning names from the House photograph. All looked well.

On the first evening of term they arrive; 60 youngsters and 120 parents. All the parents will want to meet you, some will have problems which were not sorted out last term; watch out for the game – try out the new Housemaster with special pleading or requests. Sixty boys need keys and calendars; there are broken lockers you had not spotted; you have to sort out the upper school timetable, nobody understands the hieroglyphics of the timetabler; people have changed their A level choices; two parents are appalled that the school does not permit the combination of GCSE Greek, ICT and Spanish – if they ran a school they would not be so blinkered; Year 11 pupils want to know if it is compulsory to do the ISCO tests in November; Mrs Jones does not want Archie to play rugby until October because he fell down some steps in Majorca; the Head of House wants a prefects' meeting as soon as possible (so he can tell you how he wants you to run the House) and there has not been a chance to respond to his letter, posted two days ago, about whom he thinks should be on the Welfare Committee and the Colours Committee.

Then there are all those returns due two days after the beginning of term, demanded by the Deputy Head ... when she ran Prime House she always had her returns done by the end of the previous term; who should you make fire prefects, music school prefects, who should be the library representative, the chaplain's representative? Who will carry the House basket of produce for the harvest festival next week? Has the house read the beginning of term notice?

Chapel for all 8.30 am;
Senior prefects to the Lodge at 10.30 am;
1st XV training 2.30 pm;
New men to the sports hall 2.00 pm – don't forget pencil and paper;
Art school prefects to the art school 4.00 pm;

Please could the House take notice of matron's new directive? -
no ironing on Tuesdays;
Get your dirty washing in before 8.15 am, or it will not get done;
Stop putting your feet on the backs of the TV room chairs and
Stop eating pot noodles on the balcony.

"Excuse me Sir, have you got any table tennis balls? – and Edward wants to know if there is any chalk for the pool cues?" "Could I have 50p in change for the phone, and, by the way, we could do with a third line because Fred and Harry are always ringing their girlfriends". While you are sorting out the instant requests from people and paper, burning toast will set off the fire alarm, and you will remember that understanding how to switch it off and reset it was one of those things you never quite got round to in the session you had with your predecessor.

Things do ease off a little once term is underway, but not too much. You will soon be involved in giving your Upper Sixth Form advice on their university applications, though they will also of course get help from the Careers Department. Before you know it, you will be going through interim grades. This is a good opportunity not only to monitor academic progress, but also to have a one-to-one chat about life in general; you will find out that someone has a major concern about some aspect of school life. You will find that what you thought would be a quiet evening will be disturbed by a small crisis in the house, or by an anxious parent ringing over a real or an apparent problem. Then you will be swept along in a plethora of House activities; and doubtless you will spend long hours supporting your games players, actors, artists and musicians.

If you are not careful, before you know it, you will be married to your House, which is not a good idea when you have such a charming wife as Sophie and two lovely children in Peter and Laura. You will need to 'ring-fence' your evenings off, and try and eat your evening meal without interruptions. Looking back I think I handled this all rather badly; evening meals were usually disturbed and when Alice kept referring to herself as 'Child 63', I knew I had been neglecting my fatherly responsibilities.

About a month into term you will begin to discover the difference between theory and practice. The notices which you place on the board look fine; the House rises at 7.30am, breakfasts at 8.00am, does its prep at 7.15pm and goes to bed at 10.30pm. When you wander round the house at 8.15am, you will discover your lower sixth in bed; at 8.30pm, far from doing their French prep, Year 10 are socialising in A wing, and at 1.30am the prefects are watching an unsuitable adult film on the Sky Movie Channel. How are you going to react to these things?

Toast! Always a vital ingredient for relaxation in House.

This is a good moment to mention your style of management. I received some interesting advice when I became a Housemaster. A Houseparent told me it was vital to keep the Sixth Form on my side 'so turn a blind eye to their antics'; whereas another person said he only went into the House once a week, but anybody found doing anything wrong was punished ferociously, which would ensure they all behaved themselves until he next appeared. I hope you will be a regular visitor to your house. By appearing regularly you should reduce the frequency of really unpleasant or boorish behaviour. You will inevitably find a whole host of minor misdemeanours; the Houseparent must develop the capacity to be let down, time and time and time again. You need to cultivate the long-suffering sigh. When they say "but I was just asking James about his prep" ask him what he should be doing and where he should be. Be firm, consistent, friendly, humorous, but not overly matey for they are not your friends. Never shout at a pupil, whispering can be just as effective. You must not take it personally, if you find that the frequency with which a rule is obeyed is inversely proportional to your efforts to apply it.

Before you begin the job next September, you should put aside an afternoon to discuss the House with your predecessor. I think it is useful to know his style of management, but not necessary to adopt it. The boys will understand how your predecessor operated, and they will take a while to adapt to the change at the top. You need to understand the details of the House routine; you should know all the boys before you take over and something about them. I hope your predecessor will write a detailed account about all of them, but remember he is human and his judgement may differ from yours, and young people do change quite rapidly – for the better or worse.

In many ways as a Houseparent you will be your own boss, and run your own show, but you will also be responsible to the whole school. There are some things upon which you must act, and act according to school policy. I trust nobody would ignore bullying, theft or the suggestion of drugs in his house, but some House staff can be vague over smoking and drinking, or climbing out of the house at night. Adolescents will always break the rules; they like to test the boundaries and see where they lie. But you must draw clear boundary lines for all to see. Once you allow them to get away with a blatant breach of the rules, you undermine not only your own authority and credibility but that of the school too. If they come out of a lavatory stinking of smoke do not ignore it; take action. In a large school it is quite easy to see the variation in behaviour between pupils in different houses; some know they can flout school rules, others know they must respect them.

However, it is not a good idea to be too sanctimonious about these matters. I would not go looking for trouble; I think it is a good premise that you should only act on what people make you see. There are some exceptions to that rule. I once heard a rumour that two boys were regularly climbing out of the house at about 2.00am to visit their girlfriends or go to a night club. I did nothing and the rumours persisted. Your Head of House can be quite useful on these occasions (but as this story illustrates, do not forget that your Head of House's sympathies lie more with the boys than you). I suggested to him that I had heard these rumours and perhaps he should warn the Lower Sixth that I was 'on the case'. Still rumours persisted.

I then summoned the Head of House and told him that I would be setting my alarm at 2.00am on Sunday morning to go and check that everyone was in bed. I actually set my alarm for 2.00 am on Saturday morning instead. Much to Sue's annoyance, I got dressed and climbed out of bed. Much to my amazement, as I tiptoed round the house, Alan and Ed were stuffing pillows down one of their beds to make it look as if someone were fast asleep! A dilemma; do I let them climb out of the House so I can catch them (rather sneaky) or do I walk in and ask them what they are doing? Putting pillows down a bed was not breaking any rules as far as I knew, (other than causing confusion, in the unlikely event of a fire) I walked briskly into the room and said "I have had enough of this, I hear that you have climbed out of the house at least ten times this term". Ed, who was not famed for his quickness of thought, replied "Oh no sir, that's most unfair, we have only been out twice!"

Today's parents keep in touch with their boarding children far more regularly than their predecessors; e-mails and 'phone calls pass to and from school regularly. If things are not going well the parents will soon know, but they may not tell you. I always used to try to make contact with each parent regularly when boys were new to the House. I found it valuable to ring parents in the first two weeks; each year group of parents was invited in for a drink once or twice a year; and on Sundays I would always spend half an hour talking to parents in the car park. The sooner you hear of any small problems, the less likely they were to become big problems. It is particularly important if anybody is being subjected to any unpleasantness to know at once.

I seem to have written to you at length and so far I have inadvertently concentrated on the problems you may face. While you must be prepared for difficulties, most of the time running a House is great fun. You have two children of your own, they can be hard work, but most of the time you rejoice in their achievements. Running a House is a great privilege; you look after 60 children who have a great range of talents. You would be an extraordinary family to contain a county rugby player, an international chess player, two grade eight musicians, actors, singers, not to mention children who won the school RE, Maths, English, History, Pottery and CDT prizes. It is a joy to support the boys in the House in their many activities, and to bask in the odd photon of reflected glory. I used to tell myself I was working while watching the first cricket XI, listening to the school concerts, watching the play, sipping wine at the Art Exhibition or listening to a young man tell me about the model plane he had built.

While I am sure you will find the job immediately enjoyable, it gets better the longer you do it. The real satisfaction comes when you see a small, nervous child turn into a confident adult who is a good citizen and a person of integrity. You have the opportunity to mould and guide those people who will pass through your care; a great responsibility lies ahead, but nothing is more worthwhile.

Yours sincerely,

Nick

Nick England was a boarder at school. He was Housemaster of Anglesey House at Wellington College from 1989 - 1997, and is now Headmaster of Ryde School.

Chapter 2

The Pupil Perspective

by Alison Willcocks

Headmistress, Bedales School

There is a charming tale, almost certainly apocryphal, about a busy Housemaster rushing to evening prayers one day, having been delayed by a tricky telephone call from a parent. Aware that he was cutting things fine, he rounded the corner of the Chapel at high speed to discover the chronically disorganised Tom Jones, a boy in his own House, shuffling in at the West door.

"Late yet again, Jones!" he said, in his most chastening and stentorian tones.

"Don't worry, sir," replied Tom. "So am I. I usually just slip in at the back and no-one notices."

I think we all know why this story makes us smile. One of the most rewarding things about working with young people, in whatever context, is that they never cease to surprise and amuse us.

There is another well known, and equally charming, story about an Inspector visiting a boarding house in one of the major co-educational public schools. The Inspector approached the House with his clipboard, tape measure and other paraphernalia, and just as he reached the steps up to the front door he noticed a cigarette end stubbed out on the bottom step. He reached down to pick it up, intending to present it later to the Housemistress during a discussion on House rules and discipline. At that moment a Sixth Form girl came out of the door and down the steps. A model of politeness and concern, she said: "Oh, sir! I shouldn't smoke that. It'll taste disgusting – do have one of mine."

When asked to state the most indispensable quality required by a Houseparent of a boarding House, I usually answer: *a sense of humour*. Of course there are many other desirable qualities: integrity, intelligence and a sense of fairness prominent among them, but none that will serve you as well or enable you to survive as surely as an ability to amuse, and be amused by, those in your charge. Where this is combined with a sense of proportion and the gift of perception, then the prospect for successful Houseparenting is assured. Add to this a sixth sense, a powerful (but invisible) set of antennae and an ability to survive on little or no sleep, and you have the makings of a truly great career in pastoral care.

With regard to the boarding pupils in a House it is an intriguing question as to how one best fosters a strong and positive atmosphere. What are the really important things to work for? How does a Houseparent get the best out of the pupils at all levels?

One thing is certain: boarding, as an experience, is recognisably different today from what it was even 10 or 20 years ago. We all shudder, instinctively, at the thought of some of the gruesome, dark institutions of the past, and rightly so. This letter home, which was written by one Frederick Reynolds, after his second day at his Public School in about 1760, says it all:

My dear, dear mother,

If you don't let me come home, I die. I am all over ink, and my fine clothes have been spoilt. I have been tost in a blanket, and seen a ghost.

I remain, my dear, dear mother,

Your dutiful and most unhappy son,

Freddy.

P.S. Remember me to my father.

Letters home from boarding school, reminiscent of this one, will no doubt still occasionally be written today. You will never produce, no matter how hard you may try, a Utopian community where all the pupils in your care are happy all of the time, nor where they are always pleasant and nice to each other. It would be unrealistic to aim for this, however admirable the desire. The important thing is that pupils in your care feel respected, listened to and safe. If you can achieve this, then all else will follow.

Despite any apparent differences between them, all young people have the same very significant needs. They need to feel part of a caring and supportive community; they need to have adults and friends around them whom they can trust; they need to feel a sense of belonging and that they are accepted as individuals. There are also some clear psychological characteristics of adolescents, which mark them out as being qualitatively different from the children they once were, or the adults they are about to become. They are extraordinarily dependent upon, and influenced by, peer group opinion; they tend to lack confidence in their identity; they are often impulsive; they are very inexperienced, but cannot always accept the fact; they tend to do rather than think; they often have difficulty in verbalising emotions; they may well find it hard to accept the view of authority when it differs from their own. We could all name many more examples of strikingly and often uniquely adolescent behaviour.

From this it follows that, in many respects, the Houseparent role is remarkably similar to that of a good parent. The highs and lows – good points and bad – are much the same. When parents are asked what maddens them, or disappoints them, most about their teenage children they often answer as follows: untidiness, thoughtlessness, laziness, disobedience, rebelliousness and lack of honesty. When their adolescent children are asked the question in reverse, they will say: unfairness, being patronised, being picked on unfairly, interference and intrusion of privacy. I am not sure whether it makes it any easier to know that the difficulties we experience in our schools – especially in our boarding houses – are generally very similar to those experienced by parents at home. It can at least be reassuring, albeit occasionally frustratingly so, to know that the problems of living with adolescents are universal.

We also know that the pupils in our boarding houses are capable of wonderful things. We celebrate their achievements, and share in their energy and enthusiasm. In a sense, this side of things speaks for itself. What we need to consider is how we can best foster an atmosphere conducive to such achievement and success. How do we produce a community based on trust, mutual respect and understanding? There are some really quite simple things to look out for, and some well tried formulae to bear in mind as you give thought to producing a warm, friendly and productive atmosphere in your own boarding house.

In common with all successful and effective communities, boarding houses must have rules. You will be responsible for them: both framing them and enforcing them. They are likely to be a mixture of the school's rules (about drinking or smoking, bounds or uniform) together with some that apply in your particular House. A word of warning: decide what matters and what does not. An unending list of DOs and DON'Ts will almost certainly be resented. Without compromising your standards, or those you want in the House, think carefully before you frame the rules and perhaps consider involving the senior pupils in the process. Choose your battle grounds carefully and remember, if they see you respond in exactly the same way towards toast crumbs in the common room as you do towards a bottle of vodka in a bedside drawer, then they will themselves lose both the ability to discriminate and, probably, their respect for your judgement in the process.

The same sense of balance and perspective should be brought to bear on your punishments within the House. The most appropriate punishments, and the easiest for the pupils to accept with equanimity, tend to be those which involve withdrawal of privileges rather than loss of dignity. Any sanction that affects use and control of their own free time will normally be hard for them to ignore or take lightly. Something such as a gating or 'grounding' which temporarily curtails their freedom will act as an excellent deterrent in the future. Perhaps the best sanctions of all, if they can be arranged, are those that benefit others and aren't simply negative or punitive. Again, if senior pupils within the House can help you frame the rules, then these rules stand a greater chance of being both respected and effective, owned by all rather than imposed arbitrarily from above.

Ultimately, our success or failure will depend upon the relationships which we manage to establish with our pupils. It will depend upon how well we know them, how well they know us and how effectively we communicate. Exchanging opinions and ideas in a clear, agenda-free, consistent way will be the key to a great deal. So will finding the right medium to convey important messages: remember that, with teenage children, the medium is often a large part of the message. Which statements should be written down? When are notices appropriate? When should we talk to pupils individually, when in groups, and when assembled in a House? How often do you chat more informally with your seniors? When is it better to talk to pupils in their studies and when in yours? On what occasion is it appropriate or acceptable to use pupils as go-betweens? There are no absolute, hard and fast answers to most of these questions. It will depend on the circumstances, and the atmosphere of your particular House. But make no mistake, they are all crucially important to try to get right and they can make all the difference between a happy, thriving House atmosphere and something a great deal more negative.

If one accepts that the most important things a child learns at school, especially at a boarding school, are learnt outside a classroom rather than inside, and if it is true that 'education is what remains when you have forgotten everything you were taught while at school', then it follows that your pupils will learn much of lasting worth from the atmosphere, the priorities and the values inculcated in your House. After all, if they learn the importance of consideration for others, the strength of compromise, the value of co-operation, adaptability and negotiation, then they could hardly have a better education for later life. Conversely, if they are allowed to develop a cavalier or dishonest attitude to other people's property, or a lack of respect for the truth, or a penchant for humiliating and embarrassing others, then we will have presided over something more harmful and insidious than perhaps we will ever allow ourselves to admit. The responsibilities are enormous, the stakes high and the risks unfathomable. Why do we do it? Because it is, quite simply, the most rewarding job within education.

Opening time at the House Tuck Shop to fill the gaps after prep.

At the same time, it is the most challenging and arguably the most difficult of the roles within our schools. In what other position, for example, except perhaps that of Head, could you find a situation more demanding than this scenario:

> *Rachel, a 14-year-old in your House, has been under enormous pressure in recent weeks and you have been giving a great deal of time to comforting her and listening to her problems. Her parents' marriage is rocky, her work has deteriorated, relationships have gone wrong and she has been in trouble with her teachers for a succession of minor misdemeanours. Her parents have threatened to pull her out if things don't improve. During a final round of the House one night a smell of smoke leads you towards a bathroom at the end of the corridor. As you approach, Rachel comes out of the bathroom, red-faced. You could challenge her or you could hurry her along to bed and say nothing. Which do you do?*

Or this:

> *A number of items and sums of money have gone missing in your House in recent weeks. Thirty pounds has been stolen from a bedside locker, and Sam, a junior boy, comes to you to say that he saw an older boy, Robert, taking the money. He thinks that Robert might know that he witnessed the incident. Sam is understandably frightened of repercussions and asks you not to investigate in a manner which might identify him. Robert has a blameless record and you would have had no reason to suspect him without this disclosure. Indeed, you have been considering him for the role of House prefect. You wish to protect Sam's position but nevertheless feel under enormous pressure from parents and the other boys to try to get to the bottom of this recent spate of stealing. What do you do?*

How many other jobs do you know where the really crucial, make-or-break decisions are made between the hours of 11pm and midnight? It must surely be true that in most high-pressure, responsible positions in the real world (how often we find ourselves using those words to describe somewhere other than school), people are able to do their high risk decision making during the hours of nine to five. You may have no more than two split seconds to get it right with someone like Rachel, as you look into her anxious face in that dark corridor. The repercussions of getting it wrong are considerable. It is a job where you can suddenly feel very vulnerable and very much alone. Whenever possible, buy yourself time to think. After all, Sam can be thanked, reassured and sent to bed; Robert can be left for another day; and Rachel can be asked to come and see you in the morning when your perspective may be quite different.

And then, of course, there are the parents, whose attitudes and approach so impinge on the pupils' lives. That strange, unpredictable, demanding breed who, indirectly, pay our salaries and sometimes appear to hold our fragile reputations in the palm of their hands. Not only has the Houseparent to think about handling the pupils well, communicating effectively, toeing a consistent and fair line, but the parents must also be kept on side. This is relatively easy when things are going well. It is usually manageable, even when things become difficult, if the parents are reasonable and rational and not too myopically convinced of their child's infallibility.

The most troublesome parents are invariably those who themselves find it difficult to know and understand their children. They often resort to a number of different displacement techniques in order to disguise the inadequacy of their parenting skills: over-indulgence, authoritarianism, suffocating protectiveness, a permissiveness that borders on neglect. It is these parents that make the lives of House staff much more difficult, and often Houseparents have no training for dealing with them. It is also generally true, for obvious reasons, that the children of such parenting will cause us 90% of our problems and take up a disproportionate amount of our time.

And what about the really bad times? Those moments when situations get really tough and you feel isolated, and wonder why you took on the responsibility at all? Remember that whatever has happened, however gruesome, your Head will almost certainly have experienced worse. Go and talk, without delay, and preferably with all of the salient facts at your fingertips. Difficult and undermining letters such as the following, once received by a colleague of mine, are just an example of when help should be sought. They are not as rare as they should be:

Dear Housemaster

Further to your telephone call informing me of an incident of serious vandalism and damage in the boys' boarding house, I understand that the circumstantial evidence pointing towards Jonathan as the culprit is such that you have found it necessary to 'question him closely' on several occasions. I would be grateful if you would please confirm the following:

a   He was kept in your drawing room for over an hour, against his will.

b   During this period, he was relentlessly questioned.

c   He was accused of lying.

d   He was brought close to tears at several points.

e   The sole purpose of the interrogation seemed to focus on extracting a confession.

Notwithstanding the nature of the crime involved, and whether he is guilty or not, I would like to know what gives you the authority to behave in such an outrageous and disgraceful manner. Your behaviour cannot possibly be tolerated by any parent and I would invite you to justify it to the Board of Governors to whose attention this matter will be brought by my solicitors.

Yours sincerely

Remember that there will, inevitably, be days when you feel like throwing in the towel and moments when you need real support from up the line. Try to be philosophical about the former, and realistic about the latter. One of the most telling qualities of a good Houseparent is knowing when to ask for help.

Finally, and returning swiftly to a more positive tone, I offer a few words of advice, most of it gleaned from my considerable experience of getting things wrong:

Keep an open mind where possible, and be prepared to change it occasionally.

Avoid anything that could smack of hypocrisy: adolescents hate it more than anything else.

Keep accurate records.

Walk around the house during the night sometimes, preferably unpredictably.

Involve the pupils whenever possible, especially the older ones who will contribute much more than you imagine.

Listen to them carefully; try to hear between the lines.

Keep rules to a minimum; make your expectations high; be consistent.

Trust in your colleagues.

Hang on to your sense of humour.

Be prepared to give an unequivocal, non-negotiable "no" occasionally: some of your pupils will not have heard this word before.

Why do the job? You may ask yourself this frequently in term time, perhaps around midnight when the telephone hasn't stopped and you have not had the chance to sit down since teatime; or at the end of a long term, when your colleagues are all winding down, and you know that you have still got dozens of House reports to write; or perhaps at the end of a wonderfully quiet holiday when you hear those heavy feet, the distinctive sound of raucous teenage voices and loud, thudding music from an adjacent window, heralding the start of another new term.

May I suggest it is because, in your heart, you know that you preside over the most important part of a child's curriculum; the part that cannot be examined, measured, recorded or assessed; the part that will remain long after the verbs, equations, dates and formulae have left them. The truth is that, for the group of children in your charge, you are the still point in their turning world: part disciplinarian, part comforter, part conciliator, part friend, part banker and part family therapist. You spend your waking hours guiding, reassuring, admonishing, encouraging, punishing and nurturing other people's children. An astonishing job description, if you stop to think about it. So I ask once again. Why?

Because you can, is the answer. And please keep going, because our schools could not survive without you. May you discover the depth of humour to enjoy the funny parts, the courage to cope with the difficult parts, the strength to meet the challenges every day and the inspiration to uncover something special in each of the children in your care.

Alison Willcocks was a Housemistress at Bedales School before becoming Headmistress in 1994. She is currently Director of the HMC Training Course for new Boarding Houseparents.

Chapter 3

The Colleague Perspective

by Jonathan Leigh

Head Master, Blundell's

In his autobiography *Towards the Mountain*, Alan Paton said that 'life must be used in the service of a cause greater than oneself ... if only for the pragmatic reason that one is going to miss the meaning of life if one does not ...' Should one ask an over-pressed Houseparent if they were missing the meaning of life in week eleven of the Autumn Term when there are four weeks still to go, they might feel hard-pressed to endorse Paton's fine philosophy. By that stage of term the close proximity of a tight-knit community can threaten to grind down the sanest equilibrium. Only the most diplomatic come through unruffled, whilst the blunter instruments of approach have broken all the tactful bats long since. Yet, in such an individual job, most would agree that there are no specific 'do's or don'ts' in relations between Houseparents and other members of staff. Nonetheless there are helpful hints of assistance which apply.

A successful House needs a strong tutorial team. Operating through this the Houseparent can balance a myriad of complex problems simultaneously. In schools where the boarding ethos pertains, the academic and the pastoral are indelibly conjoined. Tutors can be used in a host of different ways. The more they can feel part of the team and not somebody who just imprints themselves on a House for a single night in the week, so much the better. The need to keep sound records on all pupils, and the desire of parents to have truly accurate reporting, means that the existence of a central team well-acquainted with the House files, turns the House into the village, where the school might be the town; local as opposed to national. Good positive tutorial care needs to be more than an idle claim and the team, which is in full support, represents the quickest route to harmony. Consequently much of this essay is devoted to understanding how a tutorial team might work.

Houseparents are well advised to establish clear guidelines as to what they expect from their tutors. Even so there is no substitute for genuine individuality in a tutor. The best tutoring defies a simple set of rules, which can be restrictive and make individuals feel that, once a series of boxes has been ticked, no more is required of them. Great tutoring is an art form and the methods needed at Sixth Form level are different to those for earlier years. The one acknowledges that tutees are only partially baked in their understanding, whilst the other knows that a senior pupil would like to be treated like an adult, yet forgiven like a child; as good a definition of late adolescence as can be found. Sensitive Houseparenting releases springs of creativity in tutors, and via clever delegation, saves time.

Tutoring within Years 7-11 must happen regularly; as a rule one really solid academic tutorial a month will probably suffice but no new pupil should go home at the end of three weeks without having made sizeable contact with their tutor. Houseparents should expect tutorials to be 15 minutes to half an hour or more in duration. The style of the meeting will depend on the nature of the pupil. The tutor must find the best way of bringing them out. Sometimes it is difficult to find time to fit tutorials into a busy day but the presence of a tutor in the house doing a tutorial offers positive assistance to the Houseparent, since important issues can be fed back and often resolved almost immediately. Hence the need to make tutors feel welcome within the house at all times of the working day is important. Impressing tutors with the mission that encouragement is the real route to success is vital. An average adolescent needs a balance of at least two-thirds carrot to one-third stick; No report should ever be entirely negative. There must always be a glimmer of hope, for we should remember that we were all uncertain teenagers at some stage in our lives and praise almost always has a greater effect than criticism within the tutorial environment.

Sixth Form tutorials may be conducted more effectively outside the House environment. There may be times of private study, which can be utilised, or other obvious breaks at moments such as lunch. Some great tutorials can even be conducted over a far more leisurely lunch-time with more style and panache than is offered by the normal ten-minute gulp between picking up food in the servery and taking the tray to the conveyor belt. These can be priceless, serious moments of trust, and easily underrated. Treating pupils in a tutorial session as adults is at the core of what a tutor might be trying to say. If the occasion is not conducive to that then it will limit the chance of meaningful success. Great tutorials can be conducted on the hoof and such moments may contain that impromptu shard of wisdom, which inspires the tutee.

In recent times Houseparents acknowledge the benefit of regular meetings to discuss tutees with their pastoral team. It is good for all to hear the differing problems a tutor encounters with particular individuals since it draws attention to such worries on a wider scale than would otherwise be the case. There is also a benefit in helping to train the weaker members of the tutorial team by learning good practice informally from the more confident or experienced. More eyes watching a problem than just the Houseparent or a particular tutor can only be helpful; furthermore all the tutors need to hear the good and bad news about each tutorial group and to develop the wit to speak articulately on behalf of their tutee. Houseparents sometimes forget that part of their role is to assist in providing such opportunities for young tutors to learn and grow. Such meetings achieve this and can make a significant improvement to the long term pastoral care in the House and to the tutorial culture in the wider school community. Part of an unstated Houseparent's responsibility is to develop good potential Houseparents for the future.

In those schools where the role of Assistant Houseparent exists, this figure may be required to do more duties than other tutors in the house. This post may sometimes imply that such people are well in line for promotion. As far as the allocation of duties is concerned, Houseparents can affect the running of the House subtly by juggling duty nights to maximise the value of different tutors being around the house on different evenings. This is merely playing to the team's strengths but it does need careful steering. It is advisable, for instance, to have your strongest tutors on duty on a Friday, Saturday or Sunday. Anywhere where there is an assistant or resident tutor there is a need to make them feel genuinely trusted and consulted beyond all the other members of the team.

Communication remains a constant problem within all systems, which are far-reaching, sophisticated and fragile, like a House pastoral team. It is an immensely personal matter and every Houseparent will have some idiosyncratic methods. These are occasionally questioned from outside the House but usually praised for their success by the tutorial team that is involved and implicitly implicated with the success of the House structure. Regular meetings with the residents help to make them feel truly valued through open access to you and provide natural opportunities for listening to their perspective on House life.

The Houseparent should also have an allocation of tutees, which enables strong direct contact with the pupil body, and allows them to speak with the authority of still 'being at the coal face'. An ideal team of tutors within a House of 50 to 60 pupils will allow for an allocation of about ten tutees to each tutor. The tutorial team should offer diversity and the benefit from a balance of different disciplines. There should be someone with a pronounced sporting emphasis whilst a musician or an artist will be a great asset in matching the particular talents of the pupils to those of the tutors. Shared interests assist the start of a conversation and help build relationships, particularly when a pupil does not naturally have a point of contact with, or respect for, the tutor. The balance in the pastoral team of artists to scientists needs watching as does the expertise of those who are better with older pupils rather than younger or vice versa, or those capable of dealing with the very able or pronouncedly difficult or weak. Also having a modern linguist around is a great asset.

It is vital to play to each tutor's particular expertise and make them aware why such an expertise is so valuable, directly or indirectly, as a contribution to the career growth of a particular pupil. Tutors' ideas need to be heard even when their observations might be somewhat off the wall and betray the inexperience of never having actually lived in a House. Such conversations are all part of their learning experience and such ideas do not necessarily have to be taken up! The greatest tutors will inculcate wisdom and breadth, will be sympathetic and forgiving, and have a short memory where things are put right. The House team needs careful planning and should be worked out with the Headmaster or the senior person responsible for allocation of tutors to Houses.

When tutors join a House they need to be taken through an entire evening's duty. This way they can be made aware of the pitfalls, wise to the danger areas where discipline can break down, and can learn to trust the senior pupil members of the House whose duty it is to make the whole operation work efficiently. Great tutors conduct brilliant duty evenings without realising it, a sort of informal watchful presence; a light hand on the tiller. Preparation will run smoothly, bed-times will be observed and those returning to the House after hours will soon learn not to swing the lead. Such tutors simply rule amorphously with a natural note of authority.

Conversely, Houseparents must leave tutors in no doubt that those who sit marking work or making telephone calls in their study, are quite definitely not doing the job. Some Houses will have a formal point in the evening where the pupils gather. In younger years tutors can find such occasions daunting but such an opportunity to bring a House together is advantageous to all concerned; it creates further corporate spirit; its serves as a means of keeping an eye on who is around and who is not, and sometimes, probably more often than one would credit, something really valuable sinks in from statements made on such occasions. With the changing nature of modern school life few houses would seem to run prayers after prep, but should there be somebody willing to do that it would be mistaken not to encourage such an approach, especially if it can be linked in with some aspect of social development and growth. Lastly, tutors should be encouraged to get to know the parents of their tutees closely. Where there is an ability to address issues directly over the telephone, the Houseparent can delegate responsibility to the hands on member of the tutorial team. It always helps Houseparents to have an imaginative tutor prepared to shoulder a part of the burden of the job and thus make them feel trusted.

Within the wider context of relations with colleagues, Houseparents need direct lines to all Heads of Departments and, most especially, to the Director of Studies and Deputy Head. Much can be achieved through informal discussion at coffee break or over meals. Such times can be hard work but are often essential. There may be some central set piece meetings held by the Head or the Director of Studies. Where these concern individuals in a House, careful thought needs to be given to the preparation, that goes into such meetings so that rational and constructive, rather than flippant, discussion can be engaged. They are astonishingly revealing occasions where Houseparents can exude public ignorance on individuals whom they may not find easy for one reason or another.

From time to time there can be too great a readiness to persuade the Head to do the dirty work and grease the slipway before launching 'some idle toad' down it. Such meetings are all about colleagues gaining respect for the integrity of the Houseparent or the pastoral team. Conversely, Heads of Departments do need to feel that action can be taken at a House level if particular academic points must be seen through. Exchange of accurate information about pupils is vital to good relations between staff. Houseparenting involves developing rapport, which earns the respect of all staff and, especially, the other key important body in a school, the Heads of Department. This is often far easier said than done. UCAS report writing, for instance, is an art and there is no substitute for a little training in this and also in letter writing. No Houseparent should be too proud to seek assistance here.

The boarding House structure features a key player in the Matron. As the focus of both maintaining a friendly eye and giving vital medical cover, the Matron's role is priceless. Constant daily contact is required because the Matron will see all sorts of things at source, along with the team of cleaners. Others are not privy to what goes on at these times of day. The best matrons are capable of taking decisions for themselves and are not leaky sieves reporting every detail. Where they are encouraged to show a great deal of their own initiative, the House will run smoothly. Diplomatic skills are needed in the role because the cleaning staff also need to feel trusted and well-represented. Matron must be their vigorous champion. Working closely with the matrons in other Houses and building a close relationship with the medical staff in the sanatorium, where it exists, and being prepared to share some confidential details with discretion, improves the care and helps to set the tone. They must observe the Hippocratic oath sanely and not trade in indiscriminate gossip, to which they have natural access. For many parents, especially those from abroad, the matron is a key figure, capable of offering a sympathetic approach and thus being a direct weapon in the presentation and effective marketing of the House as well.

Good tutoring is vital.

The cleaners are equally important and where they can be included in House events, or even just invited, they will feel much valued. End of year barbecues are often enhanced by their presence where a formal vote of thanks by the Head of House can be acknowledged and appreciated. They can be key allies of the pupils and often the most surprising rogues have a real impact in making them feel at ease. Through using charm as a social shrimping net such figures will continue to get away with murder! All these unsung contributors help to create the homely atmosphere as well as ensuring the cleanliness and good order of the house. They seem to know instinctively that adolescents will be adolescent. The Houseparents' role is simply to make them feel welcome, wanted and appreciated. The surprise present of a box of chocolates or even a bunch of flowers will oil the wheels, particularly when some extra requirement or duty, usually unannounced and unwanted, has been loaded on to the House.

Normally such members of the ancillary staff will come under the overall wing of the Bursary. It is not unknown for Houseparents to fall foul of the Bursary and they usually pay for it, since under such circumstances the wheels of co-operation do not always turn. Bursarial employees are aware that they must make the whole process of pastoral management run more smoothly. However, they do not like to be taken for granted and a little foresight can do no end of good.

The Houseparent who is appreciative of all the little things which are done to improve the facilities in the House and shows as much by penning a formal thank-you letter at the beginning of the Autumn Term, will probably get more out of the staff in the long term, than the person who arrives back from holiday and rushes into the Clerk of Works to complain that a whole series of petty tasks have not been completed. It seems obvious, but it is surprising how often this idiotic approach occurs, and it can wreck relations between the academic and ancillary staff for a whole year at a time. If one has worked for an entire summer and no appreciation is shown, such behaviour is the ultimate 'turn-off'! A short letter of thanks reaps great rewards.

There are varying views on the wisdom of carrying out refurbishment and decorating within House buildings during term-time. Generally it is better to have the work done immediately rather than wait until that non-existent fallow moment which might occur in the holidays when the building is empty. Once the carpenters or painters are on site lots of encouragement, respect for the work done, not to mention plenty of matronly cups of tea, plus the willingness of everyone to mix in and enjoy the improvements being made, invariably leads to more being done. It is amazing how an extra room or two can be painted at the end of a project if the House atmosphere is good. Where a really major project has been completed within a House it does not go amiss to have a formal opening ceremony. There are odd rooms in houses all over the country which are named after Clerks of Works who have excelled themselves in delivering the changes required by different Houseparents.

It is amusing to reflect how often House space gets adjusted and numerous stories exist of the creation of excellent cubicle areas which are torn down to generate open space again some ten years later, with the advent of a new Houseparent. It resembles a series of chain reactions. There can be few more long-suffering figures in a school's make-up than the Clerk of Works and he deserves the ultimate sensitive handling. The House environment is truly important for everybody's morale and you can be onto a winner if the Bursary staff is on your side. Hence it is a virtual prerequisite to be philosophical about the frustrations of repairs or adjustments, which seem to take a month of Sundays before they are achieved. Nonetheless keep on asking!

The Head will also need to be played carefully! It is a mistake to assume the job always makes a Head too busy to be bothered. The Head may agree with Proust that 'the only true paradises are the paradises we have lost' but comprehending the essential optimism of any great school or house is vital. Heads do like to be kept realistically in the picture. They dislike unilateral decisions about discipline, despair of Houseparents who get themselves on a limb of non-communication and then cut the branch off. Also they loathe being landed with a fait accompli. The Head should be a firm but friendly critic of the Houseparent, and the same process should happen in reverse. A readiness to read through and round problems is needed; the invaluable cement of clear vision and foresight.

Heads usually admire those who stick up for their charges, those who plan ahead and, above all, those who anticipate and thus pre-empt problems, minimising their impact and finding solutions. The worst Houseparents do not spot problems brewing and generate other problems for every solution; dreary pessimists at best, or ardent cynics at worst. Invariably reactive and not proactive, they can be complacent and weak at accepting criticism. Ultimately this hinders further promotion and leaves everyone red-faced and frustrated.

It would seem from this litany of diplomacy that Houseparents must be absolute paragons with a very slow-burning fuse in terms of temperament. Clearly such virtues cannot come to the fore the entire time in such a busy life. Timing of initiatives needs the most careful planning. Anyone becoming a Houseparent should form a long-term vision of what they are trying to do with in the House, and communicate it positively to the Head. Heads will appreciate the complexities of the wider picture and will be in a strong position to represent views to the Bursar and to Governors. Equally, Houseparents need contingency plans because schools, like any other business, must run on prudent financial lines and thus the gleam in the eye project which has a luxurious feel to it is unlikely to be picked, when pragmatic choices have to be made. Developing a hard shell is good protective clothing for a Houseparent to be shielded from disappointment. Then, when on occasions the dream project does come to fruition, the Houseparent really can extol it as a major achievement.

Administrative links with central offices are a vital way for a Houseparent to make good progress. There is no substitute for remaining in touch personally, which includes the electronic connection. Head's secretaries and Registrars need constant updates on visits from parents, on contacts with prep schools, on UCAS forms and reports written about pupils, and on the increasing incidence of family changes of address, special circumstances and the day-to-day roll on of business. It is easy to forget vital details in this aspect of the job and the consequences of error can sometimes be considerable and undo much of the good work done elsewhere. Heads' offices represent the cutting edge of the business; long-suffering secretaries are overworked and underpaid, particularly in comparison to teachers, with far less holidays, and their in-trays permanently full.

Every Houseparent needs to develop an individual style. A major part of this lies in the relationships established across the entire community and the influence of colleagues should never be underestimated even when they are tiresome. All know that the job is exhausting but the continued personal interface is what makes it rewarding, quite often in retrospect! Though one may sometimes disagree with colleagues, the engagement on a common enterprise about which we all have deep-seated beliefs makes it worthwhile. Being a Houseparent is a uniquely privileged position and, whilst colleagues see it as a pinnacle worth attaining, it bears the respect of all others whether they would wish to do the job or not. Therefore, derive confidence from the quotation on taking over a House, 'The king is dead, long live the king'. The job is all about being as good the next day as the previous one: inexorable, exhausting and, when done well, deeply satisfying. As the old adage says, 'you are only young once but you can stay immature indefinitely'; not a bad thought whilst living alongside teenage boys, girls, staff and even Heads.

Jonathan Leigh was a boarding chorister in Windsor before attending Eton College. He was a Housemaster and Second Master at Cranleigh School, before becoming Head Master of Blundell's in 1992.

Chapter 4

The Parental Perspective

by Stephen Winkley

Headmaster, Uppingham School

"Headmaster", the peppery voice boomed down the telephone, "I want my son James to come to your school. He's wasting his time at school X, and after he's done those GCSE things I want him to come to you".

"GCSEs", I said, "So James must be about sixteen. What does he think about the move?"

"Headmaster", the voice moved up a menacing semitone, "when I put a dog into a kennel, I don't ask him what kennel he wants to go into".

James found it hard to settle. He didn't know what he had done to be banished to a strange school far from his mates. The first Parent/Teacher meeting was a depressing affair. "Bit of a disaster, I'm afraid, Headmaster", father confided, "Between ourselves, if he'd been a horse we'd have had him put down".

In my beginning of term address to parents I always stress that our contract with parents is now collaborative. To take an example: some home-school agreements on drugs or substance abuse reserve the right for the school to penalise children for behaviour in the holidays or at exeats. We are education professionals assisting parents with the bringing up of their children. Forty years ago I am aware that the contract must have seemed different. A small person was entrusted to a closed institution for a five year sentence, and a glossy, finished, initiated eighteen year old emerged. In eight years at boarding school I used the telephone once. Home-school contacts were tiny. Houseparents now tell me that parent X is on the phone routinely three or four times a week.

From a production model we have moved to a customer-service model of education. Where once mythical schoolmasters toiled for five years to produce something to be proud of, whether the parents liked it or not (perhaps the children who went home were not the same children, like those class hamsters sent home with a primary school pupil for a weekend, eaten or lost, and replaced with a look alike after a desperate search through the yellow pages), now the model is about partnership. In some of our schools parents choose a specific House or a specific

Houseparent. Customer-service protocols demand they should be given choice: in my view this ought to be limited. There is a limit to the number of brands of low-fat yoghurt the public really needs. But where they do choose there are some interesting parameters to be explained: location of house, age and marital status of Houseparent, profile of house, likely retirement date, these are all possible reasons for preferring one to another.

I tend to take a rather severe view of House choice: the worst-case scenario. In ninety-five per cent of cases boys and girls sail more or less bumpily through a house, but in five per cent of cases the choice of Houseparent will be absolutely vital: cases where the child gets into serious trouble, and cases, more frequent, where the family gets into difficulties. In a bad year in a school four parents will die and twenty sets of parents will separate. Parents need to have absolute confidence in the quality of the man or woman they have chosen to look after their child.

Good social relations between teachers and parents are fine, but I have always felt there is a shift over time, from a Houseparent's support for parents and child, to different perceptions of the child's needs, which may put a Houseparent on a collision course with parents. It is important for a Houseparent to remember that the interest of the child is primary. Leaving aside the human rights issues, a point my peppery dog keeper was prepared to ignore, we should defend our expertise in dealing with young people. Parents seldom have more than four children, but we have 50 or 60 at a time in our houses. It still pains me that lawyers and accountants are able to claim privileged professional understanding but teachers are less happy doing so. Everyone's had a bit of education, so everybody has a view on how it should be delivered. I was even rebuked by a parent who said, "I know all about children, Headmaster; I'm a solicitor". Houseparents should remember, first, that one of the things they are being paid for is their expertise and their experience, and second, that the customer/provider model doesn't work for the educational process because the child is not a product: the child is the client.

Of course, the primary demand from parents when choosing a school, especially a boarding school, is happiness. If Jim is happy, Jim will do well: please make Jim happy. Parents need to be taught, of course, that unhappiness is part of the natural order, but one of the ways by which Jim is made happy is by having his tiniest wish indulged by parents at home. This brings me to the important notion of the education of parents, a tough task for Heads and Houseparents alike. Of course, children are experts at negotiating and recognising the difference between school and holidays: the beach holiday with mates on Tenerife will have different parameters from a social event in a boarding house. But it is helpful if parents recognise the reasonableness of the school's arrangements. We need to recognise that we stand clear from the usual competitive demands of children "But Dad, John's parents allow him to ..." because, and especially because, we actually manage all the children and need to be seen to be establishing fairness. Thus, despite recognising a parent's entirely proper and legitimate right to be rather more liberal, we can establish that our arrangements are the only fair, reasonable and sensibly practical way of discharging the trust invested in us by a range of parents, often with widely differing views.

A high-handed, moralistic approach is not needed since deep down every parent wants their child to be able to fit in, with appropriate allowances for individuality, and without any special treatment or undue privileges. I don't know how this is made clear, because at the time the child is entered for the school or arrives at it, the fact that he may become addicted to vodka or nicotine or nightclubs or internet pornography is not flagged up by parents and may not be raised by Heads or Houseparents. When parents, at the interview process, insist on the primacy of Jim's happiness, they are not usually thinking of the free availability, in the expensive hotel where they are billeting their child, of the advanced temptations and degradations of adult comfort in the modern world. It seems to me that when the boy or girl first enters the school the issues on which collaboration and a shared view operate are much more mundane than the later spectrum of sex, spirits and holiday fun. But just because of this, a pattern of consultation can easily be set up which is reassuring later when the issues cause much greater feelings of anxiety and helplessness for parents.

Parents often don't flag up these worries because they are anxious that the fact that they have raised them may make them suspect: parents who do raise them, in my experience, are precisely those who are unlikely to let their children's lives become distracted by illicit pleasures. Parents indeed need to be reassured that it is safe to comment on the school's procedures without having to fear reprisals for their children. Houseparents are not always perfect – I used to warn my charges that I was getting a big ragged and unpredictable in the tenth week of term – but they can usually distinguish between an appalling parent and an unfortunate child.

The simple fact is that being a parent is dreadfully difficult, and if the school and the Houseparents start from this perception certain procedures fall into place. My very wise Second Master used to sermonise new parents on the skills of being a good parent. The children would sit in the chapel looking more and more smug, the parents increasingly anxious. There was a punch line – the injunction to 'Honour your father and your mother' is not conditional – but the primary message, especially to fathers of boys, is that your son doesn't need his father to be his friend, he needs him to be his father. The beer culture is an issue for us here, especially with the curse of all-day opening. What more natural for a proud father, after watching his son hammer the opposition in some rough game, than to take the rugged child down to the boozer and give him several pints in a shared celebration of the delights of young manhood (vicarious or nostalgic for some parents, and if your son can bring along an attractive girlfriend we can certainly all be lads together). Drink-sodden child is brought back to the house in time for the evening programme, a social event, perhaps, at which the school in its wisdom has decreed that some alcohol shall be served. Proud father is now back at home, while a furious Houseparent deals with the consequences of a father's folly.

Houseparents have a distance from children, which ought to encourage them to be more up-front with their judgements. As Housemaster I occasionally had to 'phone up Jim's parents to draw their attention to a minor misdemeanour by their son – overconsumption of Bacardi, a foolish attempt to climb up a drainpipe, illegal use of a chainsaw – and at the other end of the 'phone a demented father would flagellate himself in genuine penitence and incomprehension. "What have we done wrong, perhaps we should withdraw him from the school, will this go on his UCAS form?" and I would pour balm on their troubled souls, and let them know that Jim was a perfectly normal child and that his peccadilloes were part of a normal adolescent journey and that it was better that he committed them now than when he was a Fellow of All Souls. Then my telephone would ring, and my son's Housemaster would courteously inform me of some breaking of local conventions and I would stand by the 'phone transfixed with horror and ask whether I should withdraw him from the school and the courteous voice would reassure me that all this was entirely normal.

For pupils to 'cross the line' is only normal. It is vitally important though, even when the severity of the response from the Houseparent shocks parents or makes them defensive, that they quickly see that we expect the good to come through in every child and that a fresh start really is just that. There is potential for confusion here. We have two roles – one perhaps should be our more usual public face. We have an educational role and a predisposition to expect pupils eventually to come good, albeit through a pattern of mistakes and triumphs, and this should be our calm, sensible usual face. On the other hand, when things go wrong, parents will often expect the Houseparent to have 'seen it coming'. They will perhaps expect that our competence and experience will have enabled us to predict what might go wrong. Indeed it would be a poor Houseparent or parent who could never do this! We need sometimes to keep this ability calmly in the background, as a private element in our repertoire, since it is only a natural part of the parent's role to be occa-

The prospective parent and pupil are quickly put at ease by the welcoming Housemaster.

sionally oversensitive to the litmus test of positive/negative in the school's view of their child. So, paradoxically, whilst expecting us to 'see things coming', parents might also respond rapidly if there is ever a hint of prejudgement. There is no solution to this; it merely underlines the importance of a good relationship between Houseparent and parents.

The Houseparent's weapon is distance, and if he is calm and wise and honest – not always easy if he is working 90 hours a week – he will be able to steer a prudent course between the moodiness of the growing adolescent and the huge anxieties of the parents. Some fascinating unpublished research has been done on pigs bred in factory-farming conditions. There are interesting observations on the qualities the successful pig needs in order to thrive; but even more interesting are the judgements on the qualities of the good pig-keeper – a man (or quite often a woman) of calm, quiet, reassuring presence, with a keen eye and a gentle voice. Houseparents can fall into the same dangers as pig-keepers: habituation prevents them noticing routine infringements of common courtesies and one can easily say of ritualistic but habitual behaviour that it is 'normal' and therefore acceptable. It is normal for pigs to bite each other's tails, but the good pigman will always stop it.

If the Houseparent's stance towards parents and children is calm and helpful and objective, and if his wisdom makes any sort of impression, he will find himself drawn into parental anxieties where it is the parent who seeks advice. This is all part of the service, and it is important, in any case, that parents take schools into their confidence. The wise Houseparent will find ways of promoting occasions when intimate and important details of family life can be revealed, and a golfing Housemaster of some distinction completely missed a tee shot after being entrusted with a confidence which entirely altered his perception of the job he had to do in helping the child.

Once at a Ball for leavers, a Housemaster and I were given information by a parent, which, if we had received it at the start of the child's career at the school, would radically have altered the way we treated his daughter. By the same token I remember the boy who told me of his parents' impending divorce, but urged me to not keep the information to myself until the boy needed it in order to mitigate the effect of some as yet uncommitted crime! But the Houseparent must remember that in his role as family therapist the interests of the child are the only reason for his involvement. Tearful late night conversations with an allegedly injured party in a matrimonial dispute can give one an impression of godlike significance which one's daily experience does not support. But the Houseparent's calm and dispassionate presence is vital at moments of real crisis – having to tell a child of the death of a parent is the starkest example: having to tell a parent about the death of a child is not a circumstance for which one can offer useful advice: but in all crises remember that a good school provides very many avenues of support, and that the Houseparent should never think of trying to carry the whole burden himself. The wise Houseparent will in any case make sure he is supported by a team of tutors, if only to deflect the fashionable view that a child's failure to thrive is the result not of innate stubbornness or persistent sloth but because of an alleged personality clash.

Personality clashes are the stuff of boarding school life and, indeed, of boarding school growth. An early colleague, it is true, had a pathological horror of boys with ginger hair, but your average Houseparent ought to be a person of catholic views and interests. One can of course get drawn into professional misconduct if by being too close to parents one connives at a common view of teacher X, and one can find oneself implicitly agreeing with a parent's view on a colleague who for reasons of blind incompetence has failed to spot the gold beneath the sullen appearance of an over-indulged child. Of course, not all parents take a rosy view of their young, and sometimes the young have to be defended. I remember the rather rugged father who said of his son "Watch out for him – he's a right little bugger – just like his mother".

In dealing with parents anyone running a house has important decisions to make about style and management. How much help and support can he or she muster for a child? – my best ever pastoral assistant, though she was terrible at her real job, was the cleaner! How much information about children and their parents will be communicated to the support team? Increasingly I see the value of support teams, though they make the job more time-consuming if communication is taken seriously.

What kind of relationship do we want with the parents of the children we look after? Not all parents expect Christian name terms, especially perhaps, those who are new to boarding; but other parents can overwhelm you with gifts and hospitality. What levels of awfulness should we tolerate from parents? It is always a good plan, for example, to suggest times at which telephone calls are likely to be answered (a limited time is recommended: tell them they are likely to be able to get you between 7.30 and 8.00 in the morning, and between 6.30 and 7.00 in the evening) and make it clear from time to time that now is not a convenient time to talk, because there are some parents who will assume you are always exclusively at their own particular beck and call. How do you deal with parents who do not toe the line, and what means of contact do you use? The quick phone-call is appropriate for persuasive practitioners of the telephonist's art, and the letter outlining the problem and including the offer of a telephone conversation gives parents space to assimilate a proposal (don't send him back with purple hair, don't fill him up with alcohol, don't tell him his teachers are pathetic failures who couldn't get proper jobs, don't tell him the master in charge of Rugby Football couldn't tell the difference between a reverse pass and a bacon sandwich) and to think about a considered response. Sometimes particular difficulties you have with a parent or two can be resolved in a cowardly but exemplary way by the device of the end of term letter.

The truism that you can never communicate too much is important to hold in your mind when the experience of those putting children into Houses is changing and when many parents do not understand issues which from inside schools we take for granted. Try, if you can, to see some parents in groups to discuss issues: the support of the sensible ones will reinforce your own position, and it is always possible that other parents will be a source of wisdom. I remember vividly the extraordinary advice from a parent, publicly acclaimed, that when giving a teenage party you should always leave a cork in the lavatory-bowl to give prospective vomiters something to aim at!

You will end up knowing more about your charges than their parents do, because you will have seen them in a broader range of situation. Provided you do not confuse knowing about children with knowing them you will be in a position to give wise guidance to parents and to teachers and to children. You will become enormously important to significant numbers of parents. Some will remain anonymous and distant, and I remember with intense shame and regret the apparently entirely dull father of a very dull boy who came back to see me moments after our final goodbyes to ask why I had bought the Karajan recording of Bruckner 4 when somebody else's was so much better, and one weeps occasionally, but not too often, over the lost opportunities caused by a schoolmasterly inclination to pigeon-hole parents as well as children.

Confidentiality, though, remains an issue on which an individual Houseparent must have a position. Parents and children need to know their secrets are safe with you, but you must encourage them to divulge information, which might be useful. Sometimes we discover too late that a child is adopted, that a sibling died a few years ago, that a brother or sister is disabled. Taking on responsibility for somebody else's child is not a routine experience, and I suspect it is desirable to introduce an element of formality into investigating family history. There is a temptation, in our modern happy schools, to leave too much to chance in our efforts to establish open social relationships with parents: but there a number of things we really need to know, if we are to do our job properly.

Expect no thanks or praise, even though you may be a towering figure in the life of the child and his parents. Parents will surprise, and delight, and disappoint: the unlikeliest parents will shower you with praise for looking after a child who has caused you no worries (these two facts may, of course, be related), and parents over whose child you have laboured endlessly will assume that what you have done is all part of the service. But be aware that management and communication with parents is a vital part of running a house. You are in a position to help their children become good citizens; and you are also well placed to support them in their efforts to be good parents.

I have periodically arranged, at a House and at a school level, gatherings at which parents air their concerns about characteristic adolescent challenges: the end of the family holiday, the overnight party, the temptations of the outside world. Lots of good parents need to be reassured that their children will still love them even when parents decide to follow an unpopular line that they happen to believe in. I recommend these gatherings: there are great funds of wisdom in unlikely places, and they are marvellous training opportunities for potential housemasters – a form of aversion therapy.

The joys of Headship pale before the delights of Houseparenting. Helping young people to grow is enormously rewarding. Helping their parents to see them more clearly and to begin to let them go is an exciting proposition. You may, of course, wait years to see the outcome of your struggles. A Yorkshireman encountered on a recent holiday turned out to have had a child at my school, a young man now in his early thirties. I asked the father how he rated the education. "Oh", he said in a very Yorkshire voice, "it's a bit early to tell".

Stephen Winkley was a boy at St Edward's School, Oxford and a Housemaster at Cranleigh School. He was Master in College at Winchester for six years before becoming Headmaster of Uppingham School in 1991.

Chapter 5

The Wider Perspective

by Ian Power

Headmaster, Lord Wandsworth College

It is 2.00am. You have been asleep for the past two hours having ensured that all 45 girls are in their rooms, lights are out and the intruder alarms have been set. The telephone has not rung once during the previous three hours and everything is calm. Perhaps it is a dream that the alarm clock has just gone off, or is it 7.00 a.m. already? No, the ringing has stopped, but now it has started again.

You are awake. It is the doorbell, and yes it really is 2.00am. You just about reach full consciousness as you open the door to reveal Meg from the Third Form dormitory, eyes wide awake, speaking like a tape stuck on fast forward. The tape begins to slow to normal speed as your brain clicks into gear. You catch the words; "Anna has been knocked out by a 'cello". Before you can stop to assess the credibility of this statement you are in the Third Form dormitory, there is a cello on the floor, there is Anna on the floor, there is the low groan of injury inflicted, and, yes, in French too!

This is not a dream but a real situation in which you are the Houseparent. What will you do? What in your training or your experience has prepared you for this? Before you reach for the ubiquitous Houseparents' handbook or that wonderful letter of appointment from the Head ('I know that you and Robert will do a splendid job running Priceless House') you know already that there is not a section entitled, 'dealing with 'cello injuries with French subtitles'. It is down to you and Robert now and Robert is conspicuously still asleep.

Within 30 minutes you are back in bed and soundly asleep. Anna is in the Medical Centre, but only for observation until the morning, the Third Form dormitory is calm and you have not even had to telephone the senior Houseparent for advice. Perhaps most comforting is that you coped with the unexpected, without panic and made the right decisions, and yes you are still smiling!

Being a Houseparent is like no other job in the world. Many of us from time to time have attempted to devise a job specification for a Houseparent but no matter how detailed and how well researched it can never encompass all that is required of the role in a modern boarding house. Whether as detective, confidante, soul searcher or simply administrator, the Houseparent is the most important person, and the children know it.

The responsibility may sound awesome but the rewards are enormous. The qualities required of a successful Houseparent are wide-ranging but it is perhaps easiest to start with the key phrase that appears in every job specification that you are acting *in loco parentis*.

When parents send a child to boarding school they are tansfering the care of, and responsibility for, that child in term-time, totally to the school and through the institution, to the Houseparent. This decision is rarely taken lightly and in return they expect Houseparents to act as any reasonable parent would. The word 'reasonable' probably requires some qualification. Experience suggests that there are times when many parents rapidly lose their capacity to reason where their own children are concerned. It is surprisingly easy to remain rational and reasonable when dealing with other people's children. Sadly in my experience the same rationality does not always materialise when it is my own children!

So what are the parental qualities that are important for the aspiring Houseparent? Loyalty and support are the first essential ingredients of good pastoral care. The boys or girls in your House expect and need your loyalty to them and support for them. When things have gone wrong they look to you for backing. This is not always easy since often what has been done is equally annoying to you, as it is to other staff at the school. However, you have a duty to stand by them, to reassure and support them while trying to find out what happened and why.

Probably the most difficult situations that I can remember as a Houseparent were those in the Head's study with a pupil who was about to be suspended. There was a point when you had to speak in support of them, often when what they had done was pretty unpleasant. There was then the long walk back to the House and the even longer wait for the arrival of their parents. How you spend that short but critically vital period of time is often a key to changing the individual concerned and may even affect your image in the House and the success of your tenancy as Houseparent.

It is not a time to reiterate the details of the recent unfortunate event. No, this conversation is about the future, about returning to the House next week, and about what both parties are going to do to ensure that the return runs as smoothly as possible. The incident has happened, the Head has passed judgement, and thoughts and actions must be for the future not the past. Like any responsible parent you are preparing the way back to normality, building the bridges of reconciliation and not closing doors forever.

Ironically you have one further responsibility, helping the real parents come to terms with what has happened. You will have already prepared them for the possibility of suspension in the course of a difficult telephone call previously, but the certainty can be quite shocking and produces strong emotions on all sides. Parents will react in different ways, sometimes blaming you, or the school, or friends for what has happened. Strange nuggets of family history may come out that may usefully be stored away for future exploration at some appropriate time. You have a difficult job, supporting child, parent and school simultaneously, knowing that often what is said, is said in anger, and is rarely rational. Keeping your cool is essential, preserving the professional relationship is vital, and maintaining the trust of parent and child a must.

Having survived the first meeting between parent and disgraced child there is the next day in the Common Room. How will you react when your colleagues tell you what an awful girl she is and that she should count herself lucky to be allowed back at all? Will you agree with them or will you act as a parent would *in loco parentis*? Will you stand up for her and promote her better side? Will you give her a second chance in Common Room circles or are you going to give up on her too?

These are key questions since it is all too easy, and understandable, to play the hawk and take the side of the Common Room mafia. As a Houseparent you must always be right behind your boys or girls. This does not mean lying on their behalf, or playing down what they have done. It simply means putting it all into context and looking towards the future and not dwelling upon the past. This leads to my second essential quality for Houseparents, belief.

There are many ways to consider belief. In this context it is a belief in human nature and human development that is central to the role. Adolescence is a stage of development that every child has to pass through. As Houseparents in senior schools you are meeting children at the most difficult part of this transition. They will make mistakes, some of them significant and on the surface seemingly unforgivable. However, forgive is what you have to do, and what is more you must believe that lessons have been learnt and that the whole process of detection, punishment and rehabilitation will have done some good.

Without this belief in the essential good of young people and their ability to respond and change, Houseparents would be lost before they even started. The 'prodigal son' will return many times during your years in charge of a House and each time you must respond in the same charitable way. Like the parents whose place you are taking for up to 36 weeks of the year, you must always forgive and stand up for your boys or girls. You know already that the hawks will be keen to see them on their way, whereas your task is to develop their best qualities and gradually erode their worst.

There is one quality that good Houseparents possess that may come as something of a surprise. You have got to be a good administrator. Most teachers loathe administration since it seems to get in the way of the essential purpose of teaching. Most Houseparents would have far more reason to agree than you might expect. Next time you are in the Common Room cast your eye over the pigeon holes belonging to the Houseparents; for every piece of paper destined for the 'academic staff' there are probably five more pieces just for Houseparents. The same can be said for the e-mail inbox.

Schools are expert at generating huge quantities of apparently indispensable pieces of paper, most of which seem to arrive in Houseparents' pigeon holes: games lists, off lessons lists, detention lists, defaulters lists, disco lists, exeat lists, half-term transport lists, mufti day lists, the list of lists is almost endless. Houseparents must learn how to deal efficiently with occasionally excessive amounts of administration because, if they do not, then the children in their House will suffer. That disco list is vitally important to the girls in your house; delay getting it in and they might not be able to go. Forget the defaulters' list and your girls have their punishment doubled. They will quickly lose patience with a poor administrator and so will your colleagues on the staff.

Houseparents are the main conduit for information in a school. You have to turn paper around quickly and with a real sense of purpose. Develop your own systems for administration. Set aside time each day to clear your pigeonhole and prioritise. If you can, delegate areas of responsibility to girls or boys in your house, but highlight in your mind that you will still have to do the chasing when the disco list is due in. Part of your task is to develop responsibility in senior pupils. Train them, trust them to do a task well and invariably it is a pleasant surprise how well it is done.

There is some administration that you have to do yourself. Not only reports at the end of each term but the records of conversations and incidents that form each boy or girl's pastoral record. With the advent of the Children Act accurate pastoral records are now essential. Quick notes of important conversations with parents, pupils or other staff are vital. All too often a collection of apparently unrelated incidents come together to reveal something of real substance. This is when comprehensive records come into their own.

You can save yourself some time by asking colleagues to write down notes of incidents or concerns, which you can then insert into each child's pastoral record. It might be helpful to annotate these with your own notes but be sure to include the date. Never trust to your memory. There is simply too much information on a day to day basis to rely upon remembering the details of an incident. The key point is that good, detailed pastoral records are priceless, and a great relief when a major incident comes to light.

A major incident comes to light? This leads to the next key quality of Houseparents, the houseparent as detective. There are times when running a House is similar to a rather complicated detective game. Miss Scarlet, in the conservatory with the candlestick, is sometimes not that far removed from reality, and the ability to glean information and to piece it together quickly can be very useful.

The process usually starts with word of an 'event', either via a member of staff or pupils. The list of suspects is quickly assembled and the details of the crime begin to take shape. There comes a point where you have enough to make a case for the prosecution, so all you have to do now is interview the suspects and extract a confession.

The interview is often the most difficult part. It may take some time to refine the techniques and become better at the interview process. The response from different pupils can vary enormously and there is no substitute for a detailed knowledge of the personalities involved. 'Knowing' your boys or girls is never more important than when you scent trouble and when, for the good of the House, you need to get to the bottom of trouble quickly.

It is worth remembering that, more often than not, you probably have little more than 10% fact and the rest is left to inspired inference. In many situations, presenting the facts produces the desired result remarkably quickly. The usually incorrect assumption is that you know the whole story (they never stop to wonder how) and essentially honest pupils readily divulge everything, usually much more than you could ever have imagined. For others, and interestingly more often the case with girls, but not exclusively so, the process can take on a completely different perspective.

Some pupils have an acutely developed sense of justice and this comes into play when a Houseparent is trying to piece together precisely what happened and who was involved. Knowing 10% of the story is rarely enough and the process of questioning can take a very different course.

To illustrate the point I can recall one particular incident which occurred when I was working as a Houseparent in a senior girls' boarding house. A group of girls had been seen in a local wine bar one lunchtime by a member of staff. The member of staff was fairly certain that a particular girl from my House had been there. Further investigation revealed that she had been seen heading towards the wine bar earlier that lunchtime and that she was missing from her usual lunchtime activity.

House success on the sports field is still highly prized.

On the face of it, circumstantially, the pieces of the jigsaw fitted perfectly and surely Miss Scarlet would confess all?

When presented with the facts the girl in question asked the following question, 'how do you know that I was at the wine bar, sir?' When I replied that a member of staff had seen her, the question came back, 'was he certain that it was me?' As the interview progressed she made it quite clear that she felt that my 'accusations' were unjustified. How could I accuse her of being there if I did not actually know that she was there?

Even though she had been there, she felt strongly that I was wrong to accuse her of something that I did not know she had done. She never denied being there she simply asked whether I could prove that she was there! There is an object lesson here for all Houseparents; think carefully about your style of questioning and adapt it to each situation. Sometimes it will take much longer to reach a conclusion, however at other times it is surprising just how quickly it all falls into place. A touch of amateur psychology is always useful.

The most important quality I have left until last, is the quality of life. This is not the quality of life of the boarders, since that will always be paramount in your thinking, no, it is the quality of your life and that of your family. The term 'Houseparents' is often used in appointments to run boarding Houses, not only to be politically correct, but also to reflect the integral role that spouses can have in the running of a boarding house. When you take on the role you are committing not only yourself but also your whole family to a new way of life and you and they must be prepared for this.

The role of the Houseparent has become increasingly more 'hands on' with more time spent in the boarding house with children and staff, and less time sitting in the study waiting for something to happen. Twenty years ago the situation was very different. At that time it was not unsurprising to find house prefects who effectively ran the boarding side of the house with the Housemaster dealing with parents and administration. On his first day as Housemaster, a colleague of mine was told in no uncertain terms by his Head of House that he need not concern himself with what happened inside the boarding house, the study was his domain!

For the modern day Houseparent the doorbell rings with ever-greater frequency and the telephone too. There is the fax machine and the e-mail and before long the videophone. Spouses cannot help but be involved and I believe that schools must acknowledge this formally when making appointments. In the long run it is far easier and more enjoyable to share the responsibilities as dual Houseparents rather than ask an individual to 'go it alone'.

By sharing these responsibilities it is far less likely that either person will come to resent the time commitment required during term time. Working with young people is challenging but tremendously rewarding. Only by both being involved will you fully appreciate these rewards.

If it is going to be a shared role then it is vitally important that the children and their parents are aware of this. Parents in particular may be of a generation where you would only ever speak to a Houseparent. To change this perception you must show that both of you know the boys or girls equally well and that each is quite competent to deal with any issues that arise. Once this is established, it is of enormous benefit not only to the parents but also to you as Houseparents. Sharing problems usually helps put them into perspective and there are times when you need to step back and take a longer view.

You will need to maintain the quality of your life. Houseparents can be their own worst enemies as it is a job that has no bounds. You need time for yourself and for your family, which must be protected. Houseparents often find it difficult to delegate - you must have confidence in the staff who work in the house. Weekly house staff meetings are essential if you want to promote the best practices in your house. Well-briefed and regularly consulted staff will quickly form a strong team, promoting shared values and procedures. Such a team ensures a House operates effectively in the best interests of all the children. Once the team is in place you can then take your time off without fear of what might be happening in your absence. Your colleagues have a right to be trusted and may not want you wandering around every night when they are on duty.

Trust staff to deal with incidents rather than leaving them for you to deal with when they go off duty. An evening off duty should be just that. Getting back to the House at 10.30pm and spending the next three hours dealing with incidents that should have been dealt with earlier is not restful, but it can so easily happen. Do not be afraid to give tutors the telephone numbers of the boys' and girls' parents. They are just as capable of making the call as you are and it helps to emphasise that there is a whole team of staff looking after their children.

An 'incident book' in the study is an excellent idea, enabling duty staff to record any incidents that have occurred during the evening and how they have been dealt with. A quick glance when you return to the House is all that is required and you can then judge whether it needs following up immediately or can be left until the following day.

Maintaining the quality of your life is probably the most important part of being a Houseparent. You need to be on top form to deal with the many and varied situations that young people will throw in your way. We all get tired and grumpy but most of the time the young are the most exciting of company, challenging yes, but never ceasing to impress and amaze. Your sense of humour will be stretched to the limit but at times you cannot fail to see the funny side of life in the boarding House.

'And as I finally drifted off to sleep I was left with one nagging thought, had Meg's hair always been green?'

When you are asked to become a Houseparent you may fail to appreciate the significance of the question. A great deal of thought will have gone into the selection process and it is probably the highest compliment that any Head can pay a colleague. By asking you to act *in loco parentis* they are identifying skills and abilities that you may not realise you have. When the opportunity comes, if you feel ready for such a challenge, seize it with both hands and when you are totally immersed in what is the most important job in the school, never forget to enjoy it.

Ian Power was Houseparent of a Boys' House and then a Girls' House at Millfield before becoming Headmaster of Lord Wandsworth College in 1997.

Chapter 6

The Personal Perspective

by Tony Little

Headmaster, Oakham School

An ex-Housemaster of my acquaintance was chastened to be told by his 25 year-old son, "You spent more time with the boys in the House than you ever did with me". He was a first-rate Housemaster, conscientious, dedicated, caring, a stalwart defender and promoter of the interests of his boys. Therein lies the conundrum. The very qualities that make for an outstanding boarding professional can also, and barely perceptibly, nudge the family to the margins. There must be times when, to the family of a boarding Houseparent, a sense of duty seems a curse.

Lest this might seem to suggest that single men and women are better suited to that role, take note of the unmarried Housemistress who told me, "I love my charges and I am perfectly happy to give them as much of my time as they need, but I sometimes reach the end of term, exhausted, and feel that life is passing me by". Most parents who send their children away to school are, naturally enough, keen on the idea of an extended family. They wish the man or woman in charge of their children to tread a fine line, offering comforting 'family values' without usurping the parental role. Heads in turn are quick to exploit this. Alongside the pictures of happy, smiling faces busily engaged in a wide variety of activities, come the prospectus photographs of Houseparent and extended family, often with spouse, children and a dog or two to boot. Some schools go a step further and promote the idea of joint Houseparents.

The community of the House offers stability and an environment both caring and stimulating. It is a formula hard enough for a Houseparent to achieve for every pupil without having external pressures brought to bear. Yet those pressures certainly exist.

It seems one of the axioms of modern life that people feel under constantly greater stress. Workloads and speed of communication increase, and at the same time society somehow seems less structured and assured. Whilst there are many happy and supportive families, the number of parents whose marriages have collapsed or whose working lives have distanced them from their children is changing the role of Houseparent. As pressures on families increase, so too do their expectations of what a Houseparent should be doing. It goes without saying, of course, that the Houseparent's family is expected to exercise the highest moral standards and social refinement in the face of the sometimes Byzantine relationships within the home backgrounds of pupils.

We are, it appears, in the age of the service industry. In the golden age, I am told, parents dropped their children off at the beginning of term and, in a good year, picked them up at the end. These days we celebrate openness and 'encourage regular contact'. There is much to be said for this change of attitude, but contact is now made on all manner of issues: a 'phone call to consider the effect of the death of a grandparent or to complain about alleged unfairness. It has even included the trenchant insistence by one mother that it was the Housemistress' responsibility to look after her daughter on an exeat Saturday so that she could get her hair done. Not only is the contact diverse, it is also regular and speedy. E-mail, faxes and mobile 'phones have raised the stakes. It is not uncommon for a tearful teenage encounter to be rehearsed moments after the event to parents who then instantly contact the Houseparent in the certain expectation that 'something will be done immediately'. By the time the Houseparent has found the sobbing child, all is often once again right with the world.

Houseparents want to make themselves available and to help, that is the kind of people they are, but it all takes time and can be emotionally draining. The personal toll mounts as the term goes on. However understanding they are, spouses feel neglected, the normal demands of family life are pushed aside in the face of more apparently urgent, professional concerns: tension mounts, sometimes there is an explosion.

The trick is to stay sane without surrounding oneself with a cordon sanitaire. Fixed barriers in houses are certainly to be avoided. A Housemaster of my acquaintance sought peace by regularly locking his green baize door at eight o'clock in the evening. His serenity was shattered when a colleague rang to tell him that all his boys had decamped to another House. The point had very publicly been made.

It is important to accept that there is no blueprint for success or sanity. Different people approach Houseparenting in very different ways. No new Houseparent should be allowed to feel that the House is running less well than in the predecessor's time, although there may well be those who will intimate as much both amongst older pupils and in Common Room. Seeking to imitate the past is a fast route to disillusionment. It is far better to make a virtue of one's 'differentness'.

Much may depend on the nature of the Houseparent in post and the style of school. There are schools in which each Houseparent is supported by a resident matron,

Houseparents must ensure that home life remains strong.

resident tutor and a team of evening tutors covering three or four evenings a week. There are other schools where the Houseparent is the sole adult resident in the House and has only occasional tutor cover. The problems are likely to be similar, however, even if they are experienced with differing degrees of intensity. Apart from anything else, a variant of Parkinson's Law seems to come into operation. Imbued with their strong commitment to their charges, most Houseparents use any extra tutor time to enable them to spend more time with individual pupils.

The golden rule is to learn to be a little selfish in order to be more effective. I was once told that it is crucial that a Houseparent should 'ring-fence' time. Ring-fencing time may not altogether be a logical proposition, but there is an important point to be made. Having adjusted to the sheer pace of boarding house life it will become apparent that the rhythm of the day can allow some fallow periods. If the evenings are busy, take time in the afternoon or morning, walk the dog, read something utterly unrelated to school life. I was once airily advised to keep up my hobbies and academic reading. In practice this may well prove very difficult but, at the very least, time should be taken regularly away from the House: a film, a concert or a meal with friends who do not talk shop. If time to do this is not written in as rigorously as any other commitment in the timetable, it will not happen. Without breaks, a boarding House can feel a claustrophobic place, especially when the winter evenings draw in.

Dedicating specific time to the family is just as important. It is a good idea to eat *en famille* as often as possible in order to ensure, as one colleague put it, that some sensible conversations take place. This holds just as true for Houseparents whose spouses are around the House for much of the day as for those whose spouses have careers of their own. If ground rules are stated and explained most parents are happy to respect them. When the children of one Houseparent couple were very young, it was established practice that there would be no phone calls between 6 - 7pm as this was bath time. This was not only accepted but also wholly understood by parents who valued the family atmosphere in the house.

Another Housemaster made a virtue of taking his young sons regularly to a football match. This was their precious, private time. It is worth stressing to one's own children that the longer working week will result in a longer holiday when their wishes should, and will, be the top priority.

Where possible it makes sense to involve young children in house activities. Members of the House usually respond very well to their shared siblings. One of the most successful Housemasters I have known was also a devoted father. His four musical children grew up as part of an ensemble of mixed ages. Sunday music time was a high point for many in the House, relaxed, comfortable and fun. Seasonal rituals are well worth observing together. Pancake making, for example, is good for all ages, if tending to be expensive on frying pans.

Inevitably the children of a Houseparent can find themselves in difficult situations. It is probably a good idea to encourage them not to report what they may have seen or heard pupils getting up to that might annoy mummy or daddy. No-one likes a sneak. Answering the phone can have its moments, too. The youthful salutation, "Hello, Fireman Sam here", can work well with some parents, but by no means all. As with awkward Houseparenting, so too with one's own children: try and keep matters on an even keel. Do not, for example, overreact when your four year-old's vocabulary suddenly becomes rather colourful.

There can well be some truly awful moments when excesses of teenage behaviour clash with your own family values, such as wildly inappropriate behaviour in front of your young children and arrogance or rudeness to your spouse. There can be a great temptation to lash back in defence of your family. Violent reaction is seldom advisable, although there is every good reason to make your own expectations very clear indeed.

For all the grim moments, there will be many more occasions when life for the family of a Houseparent is a pleasure and even a privilege. Being able to help the young find their own way into the future is a wonderful thing, be they your own children or other people's. Your family can benefit from knowing many different types of people, being part of a supportive community, having access to tremendous facilities and, in most cases, being valued as rather special people. There are also nice houses to live in and the likelihood of domestic support, although the physical presence of cleaners and maintenance men appearing unannounced at awkward moments can create pressure of its own. And then there are the presents from happy families: whisky or saki, an evening at the opera and an endless supply of oriental ornaments.

As always, it is at momentous times that the strength of the extended family becomes apparent. I remember well the moment when the whole family of the house responded to a boy whose parents had been killed in an accident. I also remember with some fondness the moment when a rather lumpen, uncommunicative boy, smiling bashfully, presented my wife and our new born daughter with a bunch of flowers evidently purloined from someone else's garden. As time passes, of course, these are the moments that stay fresh in the mind: the tiredness, the irritations, the tensions slip away. Perhaps a selective memory is the surest route to sanity.

Strangely enough, former members of the House seem to have selective memories as well, embellishing tales of the house for many years. Take heart from the Housemaster who came close to resigning his post in the late 1960's over the vexed issue of hair length, such was the fashionably surly attitude of his charges both to him and his wife. In their respectable mid-30s, the same rebels expressed astonishment when their Housemaster recounted his distress to them. They had no idea they said, or at least no memory. They remembered their own boyish, cheerful compliance and viewed their benign Housemaster with cosy affection.

That relationships forged within the community of a House can last for life is an unheralded pleasure of Houseparenting. Not all survive the buffetings of life. It is a moving moment to attend the funeral of a 30 year-old, the victim of leukaemia, and to see row upon row filled by former members of the House. More moving still to recapture a picture of him as a teenager, sitting at the foot of the stair, and talking earnestly to the dog about the difficulties of his day.

Whilst for the boarding Houseparent relationships and pressures on the family can seem more intense, much also applies to the day Houseparent's life. There are merely differences in emphasis. Day Houseparents often feel even more of a service industry than their boarding counterparts. The working day is long and the journey can feel like an express train, a constant chasing of people and information, sometimes without a sense of the real, personal contact and gratitude that comes from the boarding environment. The breathless day can all too often be followed by the interrupted evening. Judicious use of the answerphone is a valuable asset to protect time for the family: the golden rule.

Houseparenting is a way of life, not a job. Preparedness to work all hours and throughout the week is essential in order to be effective. A tired, run-down Houseparent with a disgruntled family who makes leaky judgements or worse, drifts into numbness, is no use to anyone. A determination to make time for oneself and one's family is also essential to be effective.

And it is also important to celebrate the life one leads. In the words of one trusted and respected colleague, "a beer or G&T early evening reassures me that life for the family in the boarding environment isn't so bad after all. I simply recommend that this practice is not followed before meeting every parent!"

Tony Little was educated at Eton, a Housemaster at Tonbridge and at Brentwood, before becoming Headmaster of Chigwell School in 1989. He has been Headmaster of Oakham School since 1996.

Chapter 7

External Appointments

by David Gibbs

Headmaster, Chigwell School

Dear John,

Many congratulations! You are making history as the first external appointment as a boarding Housemaster at Fernhurst. This is an imaginative move by this respected and traditional school. School House will be lucky to have you and Antonia at the helm. The challenges you will face are considerable, but my knowledge of you two suggests that you will turn them into real opportunities to shape and steer the future course of this key House at an important stage in the history of the school. You asked for my advice and my recollections from taking on a similar position 20 years ago; it comes with my best wishes from hard learned experience.

First and foremost you must remember that you will be a unique species and no doubt will be regarded as a 'curiosity'. At the outset at least, your colleagues may look on you as an outsider and someone who does not know or understand 'the Fernhurst way', and is not quite 'one of us'. They may be suspicious of your appointment and the fact that you have known the Headmaster for a long time. I have no doubt you will work closely with your new colleagues, but do not forget that your position and circumstances are out of the ordinary. There is here a real opportunity to create something new and original. Your wide range of experience and background are reasons why you have been appointed and why you will bring a great freshness of approach.

The pupils in School House will feel most apprehensive at first at the prospect of your arrival. Teenagers are particularly conservative and like to feel at home and in familiar territory. Once they have heard of your appointment, make contact with them. I suggest you treat them as adults and ask them to write to you introducing themselves, their hobbies, sports, likes, dislikes and above all aspirations. You will be surprised what this will tell you about their characters and it will provoke many a discussion point for your first meetings with them. When I did this myself, one 14-year-old from a split family poignantly wrote that his greatest wish was to take his parents back to Australia where once they had been happy together.

Make sure you acquire the most recent house photo and try to memorise the boys' names and faces. Read the recent editions of the school magazine and any copies of their school reports. They will be impressed when you meet them for the first time and can greet them by name and show that you know that they play the trumpet or that they starred in the Junior play two years earlier. It is good to get them feeling from the very start that you are interested in them and keen to know more about them. Your major challenge will be making the handover as seamless as possible.

You may or may not be fortunate if the first weekend in the House produces some standard teenage shenanigan. If it happens this is a splendid opportunity to show (a) that you are firmly in charge, (b) where you stand on this sort of issue, (c) how you operate and (d) most importantly that you care about their welfare.

On my first Saturday evening a late night patrol with a torch round the dormitory revealed a drunken senior boy slumped on his bed. "Don't worry, sir, we usually handle this sort of thing" said the Head of House with great authority. This was an important moment to indicate something of my own standards, values and expectations. All eyes were on me. "Not so", I said, and thereby indicating that things had changed in the House, "he goes to the Sanatorium now so that he can have proper medical assistance and supervision." This indeed was justified when he was taken off to hospital at 3am! It was important for all the boys, but most particularly the prefects, to appreciate who actually ran the House and it did no harm that word quickly got round that the new Housemaster did not always go to bed at a particular time!

Do not however ignore or undervalue the prefects and involve the Head of House in your thinking and decision making, even if you decide not to involve him in everything! It is the prefects who have the most and the least to gain from your arrival and you must win them over to ensure that they work with you and grow through the experience, and not against you, which could allow them to become sour and ill-disciplined. After some years with your predecessor their equilibrium and routine will be disturbed. Some will resent you as an interloper, and fear change or that their particular cages will be rattled. They do have the power to make life difficult or easy for you in your first year and using your personality and character will be vital if you are to get them, and keep them, on side. It is helpful that most of them will be applying to university in your first term and here is an opportunity to show that you care for them and will take special interest in, and responsibility for, their UCAS application. Giving them the professional advice and guidance that makes a difference, will have spin offs elsewhere. With the help of Antonia, you will be able to win them over, although a 100 percent success rate would be unusual. They will have been brought up in a different

A casual moment for UCAS advice.

regime and you must not take it personally if some are not converted to your new approach. For them you will have entered their Fernhurst lives too late to make any real difference.

It goes without saying that the pupils are the most important constituency in your life. Do not however neglect their parents. They, too, will be slightly uncertain. They will have become accustomed to the ways and manner of your predecessor. They may have expected an internal successor, and now there is an unknown quantity from an unknown school, which they barely recognise (or worse still a school which they did not choose for their offspring). Once your appointment has been announced, it is a good idea to write to them introducing yourself and saying that you are looking forward to meeting them. If your predecessor can be persuaded to hold a party to give them the chance to meet you in the term before you arrive, so much the better. The explicit, or at worst implicit, approval of your predecessor about the Headmaster's wisdom in making your appointment is essential to help you to settle.

Make sure from the start that the parents know what to call you and how and when they can contact you. Availability and accessibility are important but at your own convenience. This is often difficult because you will be trying to tell the parents the best time to telephone without having any idea in advance as to whether it is a good time for you or not. Be prepared to adjust your advice in the light of experience. The easiest way to get to know them may be with a series of buffet suppers early in the term for the parents of each year group. This has the advantage of building friendships between parents, which can only be helpful to you – all the more so because it will happen on the private side, in your house. (Sorry Antonia, but you will be a key person in establishing your own particular style that will be the hallmark of the new School House community.) The effort will be worth it and don't be afraid to get the caterer to provide the meals if Antonia really cannot face the cooking. You will not have time to cook! Inviting them in this way will give them the chance to come as a family and to meet you and Antonia relatively informally.

Your colleagues in the Common Room will be especially interested in your arrival. One or two of them may be disappointed not to have been offered School House and may not be particularly helpful. Although your first priority will be to absorb the House, its culture and ethos, do not neglect your teaching, or the need to look outside the House community to establish links with other colleagues. They will be watching your every move carefully, but hopefully will be full in their support for you both. It is important to try and find the time to show some interest in them and their lives. There is good advice in what Napoleon wrote to his sister, Pauline, just before she departed for Rome as the wife of the new King in 1803: 'Conform to the customs of the country; never run down anything; find everything splendid; and don't say, "we did this better in Paris".'

It will help if you can invite as many colleagues as possible over the threshold of School House in the first few weeks of term. A couple of drinks parties will give them the chance to come and say hello and to see the new School House society in action. It helps to show them that you are someone who is approachable and social, and someone with whom they can work.

You will have to rely on the Headmaster and Deputies as you seek to build your own tutorial team. It is not necessary to take on board all of your predecessor's tutors. You actually have the right of veto if your predecessor marks a particular card although there is always a chance the replacement may be inexperienced or not wanted by other Housemasters. To have old hands who know the ropes and the boys is helpful, it is also important to have colleagues who are loyal to you and will do things your way. A good team of tutors is vital in the long run but in your first year you have much to gain from a degree of personal rule.

Your relationships with your fellow Housemasters will be vital and yet potentially tricky. They will be a source of support and good advice. Consistency in approach between School House and the other houses will be important. Housemasters, like Colleges of Cardinals and Cabinets, sometimes have their own alliances and sub-alliances. You must be careful not inadvertently to join a faction. You will have to work closely with them, but also you must be your own man. You have not been appointed just to be another Fernhurst Housemaster. You come from the outside and will have a refreshing perspective on all school practices. There is scope for you to make a significant contribution at Housemasters' meetings but I suggest you keep your head down initially and observe. In some schools these meetings can be quite sterile and your influence may give the Headmaster the chance to change the format. At their best however they can be creative, inspiring and thought-provoking. You have much to offer here with your different perspective and your outsider's views. You must choose your time wisely to contribute.

You will be surprised by how important the non-teaching staff are in the boarding community. The cleaners, gardeners, security and maintenance people are all vital in one way or another. You can shape them into being part of the fabric and you have a distinct advantage being an outsider. They see a lot of what goes on and certainly some things that you will not see. It was the caretaker who tipped me off about the pizza delivery man who did a side-line in drugs. But do not believe everything they tell you. The loyal and dedicated domestic is just as likely to have a fanciful imagination as the teenage pupils in the House, especially when both are avid readers of the *Sun*!

The first term will be vital as you establish yourself and set the tone. There will be defining moments when the way in which you handle a particular issue, often in itself quite small, will come to have a long-term significance. It is important that you get these early things right although nothing can prepare you for what you are about to receive, other than trusting in your own values and having high expectations. You have good experience and believe strongly in the Industrial Society's adage of 'walking the job'. This will be a great advantage at the out-set and you will soon realise that some important conversations are best done in your study and others elsewhere in a boy's study, for example, or even on the touchline. Wander all you like, for it is your House and you will be held responsible for all that goes on there, but you want to avoid, if possible, the impression of excessive prying. It is all about your manner and showing an open and honest approach. It is worth remembering the advice of St Bernard of Clairvaux to his abbots: "notice everything; correct occasionally; cherish the brethren."

Housemastering is the toughest and most demanding job in teaching. It is also the most rewarding. Taking over a challenging and prestigious house in what for you is a new school will require all of your tact, wisdom, verve and drive. However, the Headmaster has clearly chosen well. You have won the prize ahead of a strong field. I know that Antonia and you will relish the new life and will use the opportunity to build a purposeful and happy community. I hope your family will enjoy their new living arrangements although your lifestyle will change, as you just may not be as available as you used to be, at some of those important family times. Such is one of the many challenges of the job.

Good luck to you both!

Yours ever,

David.

David Gibbs was a boarder at Ardingly College. He was appointed externally to be Housemaster of Colvin House at Haileybury in 1989 and has been Headmaster of Chigwell School since 1996.

Chapter 8

The Boarding Community

by Dom Antony Sutch

Head Master, Downside School

A Houseparent is as concerned as a family to identify the environment most suitable to fulfil the purposes of the education of their young. Both will seek the best means to ensure that a child is given every opportunity to develop his or her talents to the full, as well as to ensure that character and personality is given every opportunity to flourish and to mature.

My own experience on such matters is from the particular educational tradition of a Benedictine school. In this tradition the school is closely associated with the life of a monastic community and the spirituality of the Rule of Saint Benedict. The school can be so closely linked to the ethos of a monastic community because St Benedict describes the monastery itself as a school of the Lord's service. One of the foundations of Benedictine life is the position of the Abbot as the father of the community; another is that order in the community is built on mutual relationships across differences in seniority, so that the juniors respect the seniors and the seniors love the juniors. Obedience is due one to another and, through the humility that results, a person grows to their full stature as a human being. While the wisdom of the community is one channel whereby an individual can learn what is right, it is also recognised that everyone has a voice in the process of discernment and that God can inspire even the youngest member of the community. Everything is shared in a monastic community because all are servants in the household of God; trust and responsibility in the various kinds of service are emphasised, and everything is to be valued as sacred and deserving of respect. In fact a notable feature of the Rule is the way the ordinary routines of life together are presented as marking out the road to the goal of the community's life.

This suggests, however sketchily, some of the characteristics of life in a Benedictine boarding community. It is seen as an extended family environment in which the role of fatherhood, exercised by the Housemaster but also shared by others in the house, lies at the heart of its life. Like the Abbot, the Housemaster is there to ensure that the strong have something to strive after and that the bruised reed is not broken. He has to teach, exhort and encourage, and adapt himself to a variety of characters. Similarly he has to show the compassion of the Good Shepherd seeking out those who go astray, and, while he must insist on the good order and discipline needed for the community to thrive, he needs to do all in his power to win round and motivate the recalcitrant. Even if the wrongdoer and school have to go their own ways in the end, forgiveness and reconciliation should set the tenor of human relationships in a house. Young and old are all engaged in the process of learning from each other the art of life; at the same time responsibility, trust and service of others teach their own lessons in building up the common life.

This seems to me to be especially important in contemporary education. It is easy for people today to cocoon themselves in their own small units and in doing so to cut themselves off from anything that might be difficult or threatening. The boarding community, by contrast, offers a young person a chance to be open with other people and to come to understand the responsibilities and duties as well as the benefits of living in community with people beyond the immediate family. At the same time a boarding environment provides the stability, consistency and protection to enable pupils not to withdraw and isolate themselves from others, but to develop the self-confidence needed to develop relationships and good companionship. People need independence and to be self-reliant but the boarding community ensures this can develop through a sense of loyalty to others and a responsibility for them.

Another problem of the modern professional family is the lack of time people can have for each other; time is taken up travelling to work and for leisure and social activities; parents' time at home is also vulnerable to unpredictable demands at work. This is where the stability of a boarding community ensures there is time and a wide range of opportunities. Time saved simply from travelling is available for creative activities. Besides the communal activity, simply living day and night with one's friends allows the development of strong personal relationships and commitment to common goals.

The boarding house involves several adults in the formation of community among its members. They bring to its life a distinctive pastoral awareness and sensitivity born of their experience of living with and being responsible for many generations of young people. This can only enhance the opportunities for those who are new to a community of learning how to live and work together effectively as well as happily. Indeed over a period of five or more years pupils acquire their own experience and have the opportunity, as he or she matures, of exercising increasing responsibility for others. The role of a prefect, with its demands on time and understanding for others, is an enriching experience of leadership.

Such an education in community living certainly helps a school with a Christian ethos to bring out the religious character it sees at the heart of human life. For, in contrast to many fashionable modern ideas, spiritual education has a social dimension and is not only a private concern. An environment based on the commandment to love God, neighbour and oneself can therefore give a pupil excellent surroundings for personal development. Such a commandment forms an environment in which truth is paramount and where truth is not a chilling absolute but an expression of God's faithfulness to individuals and their needs. It teaches that real discipline is based on an understanding of human weakness, so that, in a phrase taken up by the Rule of St Benedict, compassion tempers justice. No less important is the way Christianity teaches that there is room for everybody in a community. A community's variety of abilities and personalities, not to mention the various backgrounds and cultures represented, contribute both to the breadth of a person's experience of human life and also to a clearer sense of the richness of the world. This teaches something vital about the nature of God and of his purpose.

A Christian school responds to the gospel message to live life to the full. St Irenaeus stated that God delights in the fully alive human being. A boarding school environment, which includes all aspects of life and of living together, provides a good setting in which a person can grow to this kind of maturity. It includes physical and personal education with its moral, intellectual, aesthetic and spiritual dimensions. It also includes the need to learn to face challenges, to live with one's own failures and difficulties, as well as to deal with everyday ups and downs. There is no escape from any of these but the community environment will provide many to consult and offer support. A young person can learn how to have faith, to persevere in hope, and to strive for love: to learn that in the last analysis life is a gift whose value is discovered in being shared with others.

Assemblies and the formation of a community through worship is a fundamental part in this process. The opening of the day and close of the day see a boarding community come together in prayer. These meetings put the whole day into the perspective needed for first things to come first. The worship of God as well as prayers for particular needs are followed by a review of the day's events with their possibilities and demands. This helps clarify immediate priorities and to put the proper value on things. They are times which bring into focus the communication and discussion which are routine to life in the house and which strengthen the house's support and encouragement of its members. I believe that this kind of day to day review can be more effective than any sermon in helping teach the spiritual and moral values young people need to interpret their experience.

Where the Housemaster is a monk and a priest, or where a Chaplain is closely involved in the rough and tumble of House life, there are some wonderful opportunities to elicit and stimulate informal conversation about areas of experience which bear on the moral and spiritual dimensions of life. They are so often passed over either because people do not know what to say, or perhaps they are unsure how to say it. However, I am certain that young people are highly sensitive to these dimensions of life and very appreciative of the chances they have to air their thoughts with those who can share their own insights and questions with them.

Such opportunity, vital to the life of a healthy family especially during the years of teenage adolescence, is also a constant reminder that the boarding House is a living community, like an extended family. It is an extension to a person's own family; it is sometimes the best family a young person may have.

These reflections on the value of a boarding community are born of my own personal experience both as a pupil and, in my thirties, as Housemaster. The experience has taught me a lot, and I am grateful for the way I felt valued and able in my turn to contribute to the life of the community in both roles. Living with, and then being responsible for, so many others gave me something I do not suppose any other life experience could have given.

As a boarder myself I was given an immediate sense of the community as a living organism with personalities changing with the passing years, and indeed the daily changes in the moods of individuals. The natural family is irreplaceable, but a boarding community even of some 50 or 60 people was still a family experience and more. Within the wider context of the school it gave me the secure foundation I needed for learning in an academic environment, on physical and spiritual levels. It certainly helped me develop a capacity for human relationships. I needed time to settle into the community and to be accepted by it, and the experience of those who were already there when I joined it, meant that I was given enormous help. Housemasters, tutors and others who had been in the House, and had years of experience living in the community, helped me to adjust.

My own school had developed the concept of the guardian angel. A senior boy was put in charge of a junior boy while he settled into the routines and rhythm of life in the House and school. This encouraged fine examples of leadership and humanity as well the virtues of responsibility and duty. As a junior boy it meant having a senior boy as a model, and the immediate support of another's experience which was able to communicate the collective wisdom of the boarding community in a personal way. The Housemaster and tutors with their understanding of boys' personalities were, of course, also a necessary part of the dynamics of this relation-

Serious contemplation in Quiet Time.

ship. Its value was that a junior person could grow in confidence while the senior boy ensured that it did not turn into arrogance. Surrounded by senior boys with whom juniors identified not only as a group but as individuals helped each of us to know ourselves as individuals within the house community. As central to the life of the House these relationships meant that everyone was the richer for them.

Even as a boy I can recall the enormous amount of time my Housemaster spent listening to others, and being listened to by them. My own time as Housemaster was no different. The fact that the Housemaster's role is to be *in loco parentis* means that he has the duty as well as the responsibility to do so; and indeed it is usually a delight to give time and attention to his charges. Listening and being available to others is perhaps the greatest thing an adult can offer in a boarding community. If someone wants to share a joy or a sadness, to let off steam or seek advice there is someone there who knows and cares, and to whom they can turn. There will always be times when someone needs to sulk, be angry, and move through a whole gamut of emotions. It is vital for a person's emotional growth that there is someone there to share the experience and to help them own it for themselves. What is true of the natural family is no less so of the boarding community where the extra number and variety of people directly concerned in one's life can give extra help and will always extend the scope for learning from experience.

Especially for some one growing through adolescence a boarding community provides companions who are going through the same joys, problems, desires and wishes. The pranks, as well as the lessons learned while thinking that one was unique, were manifold. When things went wrong, the community provided the support and warmth needed to learn self-discipline, and to learn understanding as well. I can remember the fascinating discussion with 12 senior boys, another monk, a female lay tutor and myself. The Head of House was seeking the advice of his friends and his family how to develop his growing interest in a particular girl from another school. I suppose it reminded me of when I discussed such things with my own brothers; in this case there were some 15 people helping to prepare him for the telephone conversation as he rang this girl's school to invite her out. There was the collective holding of breath as he dialed the telephone number, combined excitement as we listened to him, and united jubilation when he finally put the 'phone down. She had accepted his invitation and in his excitement he did a sort of war dance. All the boys present felt as though they had gone through the experience themselves. But then came the time when, some six months later, he wanted to reverse the process and stop the relationship. The same gang met...

Then I must recall how one could feel the power of prayer in the life of the community. A pupil who developed a brain tumour brought the whole school together in prayer for his recovery. It was a terrible but precious moment to share such an experience of the mystery of suffering with the whole school family. It was a time when the power of faith, hope and love was palpable. It deeply united the school at a traumatic time. Thank goodness it also worked: the boy survived a horrendous operation.

As Housemaster it was frequently a joy to welcome visitors. A boy's family becomes part of the boarding community, and I recall many wonderful parents bringing all sorts of goodies for the House. One particular family would come in on a Saturday night with hampers of food and drink, from claret for the senior boys to Lucozade and Pepsi Cola for the juniors. A party can happen anywhere, but where a community lives together all the time, sharing both work and leisure for six or more weeks at a time, such events bring about a particular excitement and delight. It is a celebration of so much that people have in common. In my own thoughts, these feasts became a Eucharistic moment for me, a sacrament of the life shared by a boarding community.

The Rule of St Benedict appreciates the particular value which the wise men have for a community. One monk who often used to come to the House in the evening was an 80-year-old scholar, a brilliant man, who had lectured in the United States and in England; his own family included actors, lawyers, photographers. From the wealth of his experience he was able to share so much in conversation with the boys. A boarding community can attract some fascinating characters, all of whom become part of the extended family and bring something unique to it.

The relationships between House Master and boys in a boarding house develop beyond school. In the case of the Benedictine monk, who is usually a priest, the pastoral relationships started at school often develop into a particular kind of priestly ministry in a boy's later life. It has been a special joy to celebrate the weddings of many of my Old Boys and to baptise their children; indeed now, as Headmaster with their sons in my school, this uniting of priestly work with the pastoral relationship typical of boarding school has moved into a further stage.

There have also been the difficult times in their family life to share as well and especially those of burying the dead. Even these can be times which show the enduring strength of human relationships begun at school, and the boarding community provides extended support to the families who constitute it. The death of a young Irish old boy, who drowned accidentally, aged 21, brought me and almost every one of his contemporaries, as well as those from the years above and below him in the House, together to celebrate the funeral. His elder brother and father had been in the House seven and twenty years before; their contemporaries were there too. The emotional and spiritual support shared by so many was enormous. It was wonderful how school relationships and friendships had lasted way beyond the time shared in the House; they had deepened and such a sad event helped them grow deeper still as we all mourned the loss of such a close and admired friend.

I owe the boys who came into my care as Housemaster over 11 years an enormous debt of gratitude. I treasure the contact I still have with them. Looking back to my five years as a boarder, I know I was fortunate in the House I belonged to and in the teachers connected with it. I was privileged to have been surrounded by talented young men who have become impressive people. They include lawyers, Members of Parliament, priests, bankers, social workers and doctors, some have been in the Army, and others have led routine lives in offices and factories. Some have gone abroad either as ambassadors, or to return to their native countries where they have pursued interesting careers. One or two have become writers and artists. Most, if not all, have married and most have children. Not all the marriages have survived but there again I found myself called upon to help bridge relationships and succour those who need it. They have given me much, mainly because I have been reared as one of the family.

A boarding community lasts just a few years in itself but the relationships it nurtures last a lifetime. I am deeply grateful to my parents for deciding to send me to a boarding school. I know how much I owe to those years. I hope I have been able to give as much in my turn. Alongside others I learned to develop my own talents. I learned to live in a community and to relate to people of many cultures, styles, beliefs, and abilities. My own character has been enhanced by the experience of living with people and their problems as they crop up as well as that of rejoicing in their achievements. Having shared so much, my contemporaries still look to each other for advice and support. As members now of the same monastic community, I regularly see my old Housemaster whose wisdom continues to guide and inspire me. He, as well as my contemporaries, knows me well enough to make pretence pointless; honesty is the basis of my relationship with them. Having shared a dormitory and washing facilities for so many years, how could things be other than open and honest.

Dom Antony Sutch has been man and boy at Downside. He became a Housemaster in 1985 and Head Master in 1995.

Chapter 9

Variations on Boarding Themes

by Tony Millard

Headmaster, Giggleswick School

Ian Hay's *The Lighter Side of School Life*, published in 1914, has the ring of truth in its description of the various categories of Houseparent. Type A 'is a patronising person with few helpful suggestions on the running of the School. He usually begins: "In the old Head's day, we never under any circumstances...".' Type B's speciality is 'to discover motes in the eyes of other Houseparents'. He announces that yesterday afternoon he detected a member of the XI fielding in a Panama hat. "Are Panama hats permitted by the statutes of the School? I need hardly say that the boy was not a member of my House". Type D is the Houseparent 'pure and simple, urging the postponement of the Cock House Final as D's best bowler has contracted an in-growing toenail.' Skipping a few, my favourite is Hay's type H, 'a golfer, suggesting a half-holiday, to celebrate some suddenly unearthed anniversary in the annals of Country or School.'

In the days of Hay's Housemasters most Boarding Schools had a similar ethos and outlook in terms of their structure. There were variations on the theme and some boarding schools catered for particular beliefs and philosophies. But the structure of the majority of schools was full boarding in a single-sex environment with few opportunities to go home or be visited by parents. Indeed, it is said that the termly visit from the family, in one of our more genteel seaside towns, led to the building of the Grand Hotel. That story may be apocryphal but it does illustrate the structure of boarding as it existed for many decades, if not some centuries.

All has changed today. Before identifying the changes and diversification of boarding, it is important to reflect upon the unchanging qualities of the boarding environment. Today's boarding phrasebook contains such a phrase as 'duty of care'. The predecessors of current Houseparents may well not have recognised that phrase, but those who took their role seriously would have agreed that the care of the boarders in their Houses was their paramount concern.

The care of the boarders in our charge in a House has many facets. *In loco parentis* is a phrase which our predecessors would more likely have recognised and, in terms of parental access in the past, might have had more resonance than it does today with greater parental involvement in boarding. Whether in the past or today, the role of the Houseparent in substituting for the parents of each boarder is both a major challenge and a serious responsibility.

Parents are very aware of the love they have for their children and their responsibility for safety and welfare. The Houseparent in a boarding House takes over this responsibility during term time and, in conjunction with other support colleagues in the house and the school, must ensure that the boarders are safe and accounted for at all times. This is a primary duty of care and is not affected by time or changing tides in the world of boarding. Where it is different today is in the greater prevalence of some parents to be litigious in the event of an accident or failure to show duty of care and in the plethora of boarding legislation with which all Houseparents need to be familiar.

A major responsibility of parents is to be available to children when they seek guidance and help and, as a corollary to this, to observe behaviour and development and step in when the adult view needs to be voiced. Again, this role is unchanging and it still demands the highest level of commitment from a Houseparent. No one in boarding pretends that the Houseparent, even supported by tutors and matrons, can offer the same amount of time for individual advice as, theoretically, parents can in the home situation. I say theoretically, as there are many homes in which, due to career pressures, disinterest or marriage breakdown, the individual child does not receive anything like the support he or she would have in a boarding house.

As well as monitoring and supporting emotional and personality development, a Houseparent helps a boarder to develop skills and interests, so they leave the house, not only with academic success, but as rounded human beings who relate well to their peers, to those younger than themselves and to adults. This is an unchanging commitment.

Of course, all this individual development takes place in the life of the school as well as the House, but it is the House which is 'home' for the term and the Houseparent has the responsibility of creating a positive and mutually supportive community. He or she is responsible for the physical environment of the House, the day to day routines, the nurturing of relationships, indeed everything which contributes to the 'atmosphere' in the House. This atmosphere is tangible and can be gauged almost within minutes of being in any particular House environment. A good atmosphere is the key to pupil development within the House.

Further responsibilities could be rehearsed and do exist, but those discussed above indicate what good Houseparents have felt to be the key issues in the past and will be in the future. Today, however, boarding has developed many different guises.

Full boarding, with specific exeats and few day pupils, is still strong and schools both North and South of the Scottish border are committed to retaining the qualities of community which full boarding engenders. Mention of Scotland is intentional as the majority of Scottish boarding schools maintain the full boarding. The commitment to full boarding in Scotland is threefold. The schools believe in its qualities. Many families work in distant parts of Scotland and neither children nor parents can travel very often. Many expatriate Scots identify with the particular qualities of Scottish education and their children return to Scotland for education. The full boarding life is essential if the ethos and circumstances as outlined are to be met in the best interests of both pupils and parents.

The same argument applies to those schools elsewhere which have maintained a commitment to full boarding. Full boarding demands a full commitment, both from those who work in boarding Houses and from all other members of staff. For full boarding to be successful there has to be a full school life seven days a week throughout the term. This does not mean that every pupil has to be active all the time. It has long been recognised that both pupils and staff need time to themselves when they can choose not to be active in any sense, as they might do in a home environment.

But not all pupils choose to be active or inactive at the same time. Thus, the structures of a full boarding school must allow for staff involvement at a high level outside the classroom during weekdays and at the weekend. If a full boarding community wishes to retain its pupils, the quality and range of activity, including social activity, needs to be attractive to them.

Weekly boarding offers a very different boarding lifestyle. There are a number of reasons why parents and pupils require weekly boarding and some schools have restructured both their academic timetable and their extra-curricular programme to accommodate this style of boarding. Some choose it because both parents have demanding careers but still wish regular contact with their children at the weekends to provide the opportunity for contact which week-day time cannot offer. This is considered to be the shape of the Millennial family. Many families have both parents with challenging careers and weekly boarding schools can cater for such needs.

Some choose weekly boarding because the nature of daily journeys, both to and from school, and out of school activities mean that an inordinate amount of time is spent in a car. Many families have done their sums and acknowledged that weekly boarding is a better option, both in terms of the family budget and the effective use of family time for both parents and children.

When occasionally challenged by journalists on the 'inhumanity' of boarding, especially the weekly variety, as a 'convenience for parents who should never have had children in the first place', I do inquire of them the quality of their family life. Is one parent always available to meet the children from school and be at home on their return from school for the rest of the evening? Is one parent always available to offer transport and support for all of the children's extra-curricular activities? Is one parent always available to help with homework? Does the family eat together every evening and have discussion over the meal rather than watch television as the regular accompaniment to meals? Market research shows that most families, unlike those shown in the breakfast adverts, rarely eat together and only get together to discuss and relate in the car when the individual computers, televisions and stereo players are not available.

Those who seek to challenge the ethos of boarding, in whichever boarding configuration, have more often than not never visited a modern boarding school and base their accusations on hearsay or prejudice. In addition, they do not wish for their own family values to be challenged in comparison to what boarding offers on a full or weekly basis.

Weekly boarding has a different set of challenges to full boarding. Weekly boarding puts constraints on the timetable and the working week. Without weekend life, even if there are sports fixtures, so much more has to be fitted into five days. There is also the challenge of rebuilding the community of the boarding House every Sunday evening or Monday morning if the majority of the house has spent the weekend at home. That majority, of course, can leave a minority in a house in a school, which accepts full boarders as well as weekly. This is a real challenge for the school and the Houseparent and pastoral team. Unlike the seven day commitment of all staff in a full boarding school, the Houseparent is reliant on a team to create an environment which is also appealing to the full boarders. It is noticeable that in the dissertations for the Boarding Schools' Association Certificate of Professional Practice in Boarding there are a growing number which concentrate on the proper weekend provision for weekly boarders.

The diversification of boarding has brought its own challenges but also its new markets. One new market is in flexi-boarding where pupils and their families may opt for boarding almost on an ad hoc basis. Whilst this has brought its logistic challenges it has also brought new boarders, in a new definition of the word, into the system. In a school which has flexibility in its boarding, it can provide an overnight boarding experience either out of a pupil's curiosity about boarding or because of a parental need to be away or after a late night school expedition when the offer of

Duet rehearsal for the House Concert.

overnight boarding is made. There is much evidence of day pupils 'converting' to boarding from such an experience.

It is worth confirming at this point that most boarders board out of personal choice. The Director of the Boarding Schools' Association visits over 50 boarding schools a year and one of his first questions to boarders is just who made the choice to board. In about 90% of cases, it is the pupil's choice. That is another useful statistic when in conversation with journalists who hold their own preconceptions of our school world.

There have also been changes in the structure of boarding houses. Traditionally a Senior School house was for pupils aged from 13 to 18 or 11 to 18. Many houses still have this structure, but there has been a move away from this in the last two decades to the provision of specialist Sixth Form houses for the two years before university.

This development is not surprising. The Sixth Form is an area where there is intense competition both within and outside the independent sector. Sixth Form Houses have been developed for a variety of reasons. Rightly, many have thought that Sixth Form Houses help the process of maturing and provide a better atmosphere for A Level study. This arrangement also suits those who believe that the 13 to 16 or 11 to 16 is a more cohesive boarding group and that younger pupils can feel overwhelmed by the presence of Sixth Formers in the House.

In some schools Sixth Form Houses have been developed as a marketing strategy to attract pupils to stay in the school after GCSE. The bonuses are obvious. The Sixth Form House is a pre-university environment where a Houseparent can concentrate energies on developing particular strategies for Sixth Form pupils: study habits, self-motivation, time management, career discussion, university applications, management of self in terms of domestic chores and cooking. All these are essential for a successful university career and it is worth noting the significant numbers of pupils who choose to become boarders in the Sixth Form to avail themselves of this pre-university training.

The existence of a Sixth Form House or Houses brings its own challenges. How is the prefectorial system managed in a House where the oldest pupil is 16? How do the Sixth Form pupils relate to the whole school when they are living separately in a House with its own particular mores and a less structured environment? Schools have faced these challenges and found interesting solutions, which have added to the dynamic of the boarding community.

There has been no bigger challenge in boarding than the large expansion in co-education. The strengths of each system can be articulated but both single-sex and co-education boarding schools have their own challenges.

The single-sex boarding school knows it must address the social and cultural challenges produced by a single-sex environment. Many novel strategies have been developed to ensure that the perceived qualities in academic terms in a single-sex environment are not overshadowed by a lack of social opportunity in terms of personal development.

Equally boarding schools which have decided to become co-educational, and they are, with only one or two notable exceptions, schools which previously only took boys, have their own pressures. The boarding requirement in a co-educational school must ensure the appointment of boarding staff who are skilled in understanding both sexes, especially in a mixed house. Whilst it might be assumed that the co-educational environment automatically offers opportunities for social development in a mixed environment, this is not always the case. Care has to be taken to ensure that social development is not a greater priority than academic or extra-curricular development.

Boarding schools today are much more aware that they need to analyse their strengths and decide what style of boarding will be suitable to their market. In boarding as it is structured today, a school cannot be all things to all parents or pupils. The principles behind some boarding environments are in direct conflict with others. Any school or House must assess its own market and strengths to ensure that the energies, in terms of boarding, are channelled into the right style of boarding for the school or the House.

And what of the future?

Despite the downward trends shown in the Annual ISIS Census on Boarding there has been a major investment in boarding. The Autumn 1999 ISIS *News* article on Boarding revealed investment in new Houses and refurbishment in the millions of pounds. No Governing Body would be committing such funds unless they were certain of the future of boarding. But there is a 'but'. If the boarding market is shrinking it is clear that only those schools with a distinct commitment to boarding will be able to continue to offer boarding education. Such commitment is twofold.

First, there is the commitment to the boarding environment. The era of 'rough is good for the character' is dead. As well as pupils, mothers choose boarding and boarding schools. The *en suite* boarding house is not a dream: it is here. The Director of the BSA has seen three houses with en suite facilities and many more are on stream: not just en suite but with personal e-mail and telephone facilities in some cases and, certainly, e-mail facilities aplenty in the house. A house may not be a home but the new boarding house is as close to a pupil's home bedroom as one could ever imagine. Indeed, as one parent said to me as I was visiting a school, this room is better than he has at home. An interesting comparison is that boarding facilities are far superior to almost all university rooms. Thus, it is clear that new boarding houses will continue to offer a high standard of accommodation and facilities and probably continue to set trends.

Secondly, and no less important, there is a commitment to professional staffing. That is not to say that boarding colleagues in the past were not professional. They were, but we are entering a new age where professional qualification is key in any career and none the less so in boarding education.

Boarding legislation is extensive and complicated. The National Committee for National Boarding Standards is composed of members of the five ISC School Organisations, the State Boarding Schools, ISC, ISIS, the Independent Schools Bursars Association, the Department for Education and Employment, the Department of Health, Service Children's Education, Ofsted, Local Authorities (represented by Oxfordshire County Council), Medical Officers of Schools Association and the Boarding Schools Association. Their work is well advanced and the National Boarding Standards they adopt will be considered by Government and are very likely to be adopted as the National Boarding Standards. Boarding staff need to be very aware of the extent, implications and legal requirements of these standards.

This is where the Professional Development Programme of the Boarding Schools' Association is so significant. The Association has 300 boarding staff training at any one time, studying for the university-validated Certificate of Professional Practice in Boarding Education. It also has a rolling programme of Day Conferences on Boarding Legislation with particular emphasis on Child Protection. Individual schools can organise INSET training with the BSA on a topic particularly relevant to their boarding development. All these training programmes are financially supported and endorsed by the Department for Education and Employment.

There is a growing set of boarding publications and the BSA Website is developing as a communication tool for BSA members. The BSA organises 10 conferences a year and these are a good opportunity for boarding staff to meet together, train together and share good practice. They are times of learning and sharing, a great opportunity to come together from what can sometimes be a lonely professional role.

All Heads know that the lifeblood of a boarding school is those colleagues and the tutorial teams who look after the Houses. "Duty of care" has not changed in centuries except that today boarding is a transparent environment visited by parents, inspectors, journalists and prospective pupils. The Houseparent's work has not become any easier but there is professional support and the age-old satisfaction of seeing young people becoming valued and developing into valuable adults in our ever-demanding society.

Tony Millard was Housemaster at Wells Cathedral School before becoming Headmaster of Wycliffe College in 1986. In 1993 he became Headmaster of Giggleswick School. He is also currently Chairman of the BSA.

Chapter 10

Vines and Fig Leaves –
The Co-educational Perspective

by Michael Mavor

Head Master, Rugby School

Just before Rugby School took its first 13-year old girls in September, 1993 I announced some changes to the rules for visiting between Houses. They became less liberal. One Sixth Form boy, possibly used to persuading a junior to lend him his study for a Platonic chat about prep with a visiting Sixth Form girl (study bedrooms were always off limits), came to see me to complain. He did so with articulate force. When I refused to budge, he went to the study door, grinned (I think) and said; "Sir you are wrong but I will say this for you; you are consistent ..."

Consistency is important in a co-educational school but I assume, too, that most of my observations will already be well known by Houseparents in single-sex schools. There are schools in which Houseparents do not teach, but mostly Houseparents are graduates who are appointed for a set term on a reduced timetable with some support staff to look after 50 to 60 pupils. Some will have served as Assistants or Resident Tutors in a House but all should have attended the HMC Training Course and have received and read the School handbook for new Houseparents, just as Heads are known to wolf down the HMC Manual of Guidance in preparation for their task ...

At a School at which I once worked a new Housemistress was asked if the smoking evening could be changed to Wednesdays; her predecessor, the girl said, had always insisted on Fridays! Other training might include attending an Inset day at the School, or having a mentor as well as a Senior Houseparent in whom to confide, and then having and continuing to have, with colleagues who run Houses, an Away Day after half-term in the Summer to eat, drink and throw around some ideas. One HMC School is currently lucky enough to have parents who provide their castle for 24 hours for this purpose. Meals and wine are provided (though the School pays for these) and the Houseparents decide for themselves who sleeps in the dungeon.

Heads need to do their best to provide every reasonable support for men and women who are running Houses. There are several different ways in which a

House can be run well, and even inspirationally, and the challenge to Heads is to nourish a consistent core while welcoming bright planets, even if their orbit is elliptical. Equally Houseparents, while enjoying their differences, must recognise that they and the Head, too, are all musketeers.

There are different models of adult care. In some schools every boarding House has an assistant Houseparent or resident Tutor. There are matrons, resident or living out, and in some cases Houses have assistant matrons too. This helps with regard to time off for matrons and with adult cover generally throughout the week. Houseparents might have a half-day off each week and two weekends a term in addition to the Leave-out weekends. Tutors in each House can do one evening's duty on a regular rota basis so that the Houseparent is part of a team on two or three evenings each week rather than always being in the front line. There must be substantial secretarial help for the excess of paper – some of it generated by the Head.

Half-terms are now often longer in the Autumn and Summer Terms and the Lent Term can be usefully divided into three 3½ week sections by a three-night and a four-night Leave-out weekend. This does not thrill the skiers but it makes the term much easier for everybody, particularly for the resident staff. Usually the two Leave-out weekends in the Autumn Term are of two nights and everybody must leave the School. I do not identify any of this as the only recipe but simply as a way of recognising that running a House for boys or girls is a tough assignment. The pay reflects this too: the allowances and benefits for running a House can amount to about £14,000 on top of the salary at 1999 levels.

All of this is meant to release Houseparents to do what they are appointed to do. I once caused a colleague to go white with imminent fury when he asked me what I thought was the most important thing he did as a Housemaster "I don't know," I replied and then quickly went on to say that I thought that the most important thing any Houseparent did was always unseen and frequently unknown: to listen, wander, discuss and talk.

The strain can be considerable and the Head needs to ensure that there is a Senior Houseparent in whom others can confide and who can also quickly have the Head's ear if real anxieties are developing in any area. There should probably be a cycle of appraisal with a really major one every three years, one that concentrates on the teaching in another year and a mini-appraisal in the other. This means that Houseparents have a chance to talk about things formally on an annual basis as well as in all the other informal ways. A detailed annual written report to the Head is also helpful; this could cover recruitment, tone and atmosphere, academic results, cultural life, sport, Tutors and Matrons, budgets, the fabric and structure of the House, the Houseparent's own situation and ambitions for the future and targets for the coming year as well as for the next five years. This report should go hand-in-hand with an hour's tour of the House by the Head and the Estates Bursar.

Kurt Hahn once said, "we must molest the contentedly unfit." This surely does not apply to Houseparents – but they nonetheless need sleep, exercise and refreshment like the rest of us and should be given the chance to take it.

Both Heads and Houseparents need – for their Schools and Houses respectively – a sense of the resonance of life, even and possibly even particularly in a school. That resonance is always related to discipline, self-discipline and sometimes even to the unpredictable harshness of outside events, but must always sound beyond it and exist in a time frame that lifts itself from the routine.

I am writing this in New York, where nobody wears a poppy, in the week running up to Remembrance Sunday. My brother once occasioned a loud family argument at lunch in the George Hotel in Perth when he announced (he was 17 and I was 12) that we would never have won the war without America. My father exploded – he had been lucky enough to survive 3½ years under the Japanese in Changi Gaol and felt the strongest possible loyalty towards the British and the Australians – which he then made very clear to the other 42 people having lunch. Right now I happen to be reading Eric Lomax's *The Railway Man*. Lomax grew up in Edinburgh as I did, loved the locomotives of Waverley Station, but was in Changi and survived working on the Burma/Siam railroad. In *The Railway Man* he talks both of the British military habits that somehow help in the face of profound difficulty and of the simple, savage atrocities that the outside world sometimes brings upon us:

There were now about 18,000 of us left. A new Japanese commander had been appointed, General Fukuye Shimpei, and he made his mark by issuing an order that every remaining POW had to sign a 'non-escape form'. Only four prisoners signed. To show us that he meant to be taken seriously, Fukuye shot four prisoners on the beach near Changi. Allegedly, they had tried to escape. Of course we heard about all the cruel details; Fukuye intended that we should. He had ordered Colonel Holmes, our most senior remaining officer, to appear on the beach in the late morning of 2nd September with six of his colleagues. The four POWs were tied to posts in the sand; a firing squad of members of the Indian National Army, the renegade nationalist force supported by the Japanese, were led out in a calculated piece of political theatre. British soldiers were to be shot by their former subjects. The first shots failed to kill them; slow volleys finished them off as they lay on the bloody sand.

I have never done military service but when I was appointed a Head my Headmaster from my schooldays suggested that I spend a day with an Army adjutant. I thought he was half-mad, which is generally the view that boys and girls have of their Head and possibly even of their Houseparent, but later realised how wise he was. Adjutants can teach you some wonderful systems for just about everything – and these work even when half your men are dead or, as in the more peaceful context of the School, when, at the end of a long term, all of your men and women are half-dead. The men in Malaya and Changi held themselves together with certain routines and self-discipline. The same applies in a totally un-military way to Houses. In a co-educational school there is always a balance to be struck between a general belief in hierarchy and tradition in boys' Houses and a more open atmosphere in girls' Houses. The middle road is probably the right one but, as in all matters, School Prefects and Houseparents need to learn from each other, perhaps by spending at least a day in each other's Houses just to see how things are done.

Armies march on their stomachs and boys and girls are not very different. The Head needs to ensure that the same choice and quality of food is available in all Houses. Thought needs to be given, too, to things like queues (senior pupils, Houseparents and the Head should wait their turn), clearing, family or cafeteria style service and so on. Where there is central feeding most of these things become easier to deal with in theory but the no man's land of a refectory carries its own dangers. Girls' Houseparents need to know whether there has been any previous history of anorexia and always to watch out for that and to keep the Head informed. There is the odd anorexic boy but I have never known one; indeed in my first English class last term an ample boy from Bermuda offered me a chocolate ...

The same consistency applies to visiting arrangements, common rooms, opportunities for outings and the physical structure of the Houses. I reckon that the ideal House should number no more than 55, that the Head must, wherever possible, ensure a programme of refurbishment that creates single study-bedrooms (in a 13-18 school) for all except the first year, who should be in two small dormitories with a senior pupil in an adjacent study-bedroom and that while Houses need to nourish their own identity with regard to drama and music there should be as much sharing and co-operation between boys' and girls' Houses as possible.

There are always lots of social events in a co-educational school and Houseparents and the Head need to make sure that the same people are not always receiving the invitations. School events have to be very carefully managed and supervised; House events, because of the ownership, nearly always go extremely well. Dances and parties that involve year groups are often very successful. The School needs a policy too, on the dreaded public displays of affection; note that I am not going into any detail. I am simply a tapper of shoulders and shiner of headlights but I do know when to do that!

As in all areas, Houseparents and their Houses benefit from clearly understood and stated rules and guidelines about sexual behaviour. Schools should have clear policies, too, on bullying, drugs, drink and smoking. Days of preventative effort in the area of decent and inclusive behaviour in year-groups and throughout the school are worth the time; Heads and Houseparents who work at this will help their schools to be places in which the smaller executions of peacetime do not take place. Last – and the last should be first – as most boys and girls go to school to work, why should there not be a commonly understood policy and contract with regard to that, too? Boys and girls across the school need to know where they stand with regard to prizes, distinctions, commendations, choices of subjects, preparation, behaviour in class, detention, sloppy work and so on – and so do the staff.

While I believe in a system that delegates daily and weekly responsibility for supervision of academic progress to a House Tutorial team and the Director of Studies, the Houseparent must place academic matters very high on the list of priorities and be well informed about them and the Head must make sure that this is consistent across the School. It is worth keeping examination statistics for boys and girls and for each House. Of course girls across the country do better at GCSE, boys catch up at A Level and we men overtake women at the age of 80; the last is a prediction, not a statistic.

Nonetheless we should look for equality and consistency in most areas. The entry policy of a co-educational school needs to give boys and girls and brothers and sisters an equal chance provided that they meet the entrance standard.

Sometimes Heads and Houseparents are involved in the challenging process of taking the first step towards co-education or of increasing the ratio of girls to boys and converting one or more boys' Houses to girls' Houses. There are certain things to remember in such circumstances.

First the philosophy must be right even if the business side of things plays a part, as it nearly always does. Why and to what extent should the School become a co-educational one? That question will probably have been discussed openly with the Common Room and the Governing Body and less openly (perhaps sometimes in response to a question at lunch when one's mouth is full of spaghetti) with the boys. The answer needs to be a convinced and convincing one. Co-education changes a School dramatically though the sea-changes may take time and all of

End of term: All packed and ready for home.

that needs to be thought through so that the School, in its own particular context, has considered the curriculum, games, music, drama, art, uniform, visiting arrangements, social life, hierarchies and leadership, toilets, computer facilities, handbasins and electric sockets...

The announcement of the first step to co-education requires detailed and personal communication with boys, parents, teaching and non-teaching staff, governors, Old Boys, and their committees, prep schools, the press and possibly even the local butcher. A second move to greater numbers of girls requires less philosophy but just as much precision.

Which boys' House (or Houses) is to be converted? No doubt a small and trust-worthy working party will have looked at the field, taking into account such things as the history, structure, location and tone of the House, the due date for a change of Houseparent, the need for refurbishment, and so on. The financing for a move to co-education, however, should always include as much money as possible for boys' Houses.

Careful planning needs to be done in advance over the winding down of a boys' House; how can morale and (wherever possible) numbers be kept up and choice be offered for what always at first, particularly in a House-based school, seems a dis-aster? Will the School need an annexe? What are the staffing implications? – and here one must remember cooks, matrons, cleaners, gardeners and handymen. What are the implications for the operating account and for capital expenditure?

Before D-Day a plan for the proceeding fortnight or so needs to be prepared. There will be dozens of different versions of the same detailed but unmuddled let-ter for parents of different year-groups in the House, for staff, prep schools, par-ents whose sons are registered for that House, parents in general, present and future, the Old Boys and their central committee – and so on. These letters need to be posted on D minus one and faxed on D-Day to parents who live abroad. Secretaries need to be discreet (and they deserve a party afterwards) and the frank-ing machine, xerox and envelope-stuffer all need to be working. A press statement needs to be prepared. Staff who are going to be most affected have to be seen in person at the latest possible point.

On the day itself the Head needs to speak face-to-face with the boys' House(s), then to the Common Room, then to the School. First time round Heads and Houseparents can expect almost any response, from silence to boycotts, from tele-phone calls to newspapers to black armbands, from genuine good humour to raw anger. As well as writing to the parents concerned, the Head, Houseparent and Registrar should telephone the parents of those most directly affected – those who will still be in the School when the change happens and those who are about to come to the House(s). These parents are the ones who feel the most let down. It is worth drawing the fire by holding a meeting for the parents and it may be helpful to have the Chairman of Governors present. On D-Day visits also need to be made to the domestic staff so that they know what you have worked out for them. Though all of this requires fortitude it also benefits from a reasonable cheerfulness and brightness of heart. With a bit of luck, foresight and experience of working in a team, Heads and Houseparents will be giving the same message. In due course boys and girls will be saying at an early stage that they want to come to a School where real care has been taken over the move to co-education (about which there is much more to be said!).

The whole area of recruitment, whether it is done on a School or a House basis, is crucial. Houseparents need to be advised how parents (and young boys and girls) form impressions on a visit; they need to be given every chance to talk to the pupils in the House and if the House is a well run and happy one, that will show. Courtesy and manners are important – and Houseparents, too, need to keep in touch with prospective parents in whatever form they think suitable and to liaise with the Central Registry over this. Just as the House is home for the pupils in it and treats, trips, chocolate (hot or cold) and sometimes a meal on the private side are important, parents also need to be given a warm welcome (at the beginning of each term it is not a bad idea for the Houseparent to stand in a place passed by most parents) to House plays, music evenings and so on, and invited to drinks or supper.

Similar policies should exist across the school for House Prefects and identical ones for School Prefects. There should be an equal chance for a girl to be Head of School or there should be joint Heads of School, a better arrangement, I think than Head Boy and Head Girl, which can suggest that the two look after their own. I believe that women should run girls' Houses and men boys' Houses but I guess that every rule is there to be broken.

Heads and Houseparents need to remember too, that arrangements for day-pupils have to be different in some areas. If there are separate Houses for day-pupils it may seem that the Houseparents of these Houses have an easy time of it in the evenings and on Saturday nights – but one should remember that there are 50 or 60 sets of parents making helpful suggestions on the telephone and in writing, dodging chapel and slipping their sons and daughters away to play in the local rugby, soccer or tennis teams. Heads need to give all the help they can to these Houseparents to ensure that day pupils are never second-class citizens; sport can be helpful here and there should be entirely satisfactory arrangements for eating and staying on in the evenings for rehearsals, performances, debates or social events.

Houseparents sometimes feel that nobody really understands quite what their life is like. That may sometimes be true and the least we can do as Heads (Heads who have been Houseparents in their time probably have a sensibly short memory) is to do an evening's duty each term in sole charge of a boarding house with the occasional Saturday night thrown in. The trouble from the Houseparent's point of view is that this is rather like cooking: done infrequently it is great fun...

Heads, Houseparents, matrons and the medical team must have sensible lines of communication and action both amongst themselves and with parents for anything from 'flu to broken limbs, appendicitis, glandular fever and acne. The health of pupils is a matter of enormous trust by parents and we have to get it right.

When a Head talks to a new Houseparent right at the outset every encouragement should be given to share problems or misgivings with the Head – or with the mentor or the Senior Houseparent or just another colleague who is running a House. It can be very wearing to have a resident thief or a seam of unpleasantness in a House but the solution often seems easier once the facts and the issues have been shared and discussed. That does not have to be done in a study.

An experienced Headmastering colleague once gave me four questions to ask myself in any situation:

> What are the facts?
> What are the issues?
> What am I going to do?
> Who do I have to tell?

Those are four good questions for Houseparents, too, and the fourth causes more problems than any other. Houseparents need to know what the Head wants to hear or read and when. The Head needs to advise his colleagues how and when to communicate with their pupils and parents as well as with colleagues in the Common Room and with feeder schools. There are routine things and intuitive things; parents always appreciate a brief postcard when their son or daughter has done particularly well at something and a telephone call if something is not going so well – and if the Head is briefed about it he/she has a greater chance than usual of saying something sensible on encountering the parents. It makes sense, too, to send copies of the House Report to the Prep School Head at the end of a pupil's first term; even better if the Houseparent can find the time to write an accompanying note. GCSE and A level results are usually welcome too, and to look at the other side of things, careful notes have to be taken of any complex or difficult telephone conversations.

A little while ago I went to a prep school to give a sermon at the evening service. I had never been there and after a friendly cup of tea wandered round the school on my own to try to glean a little of its soul. In one classroom there was a messianic game of soccer going on but one boy sat unmoved behind a desk in the centre of the room except that he was writing lines; 'Je dois faire attention en classe.' I asked him whether he had fallen asleep in French. 'No, sir' he replied, 'I head-butted my friend.'

War is always possible. When it breaks out in whatever form, I hope that Houseparents will want the support of the Head. Houseparents, who quickly get engulfed in the next thing, might remember too, that a Head's heart is warmed by a sentence of thanks, a cup of coffee in the kitchen, a chuckle or smile when support has been given, and that the Head, too, can be deeply grateful for a word of support on a pavement or touchline when he/she has taken a head-butt or two in a good cause.

I have been a Head for a while now but was never a Housemaster; that, and the evidence of this article, might make me doubly dumb. I have had the pleasure, however, of appointing and working with a fair number of men and women in their Houses and it is the combination of a sensible routine and discipline with a sounding of resonance that makes for the best in both Head and Houseparent. I suppose I might have been a Housemaster as well as Headmaster but my predecessor stopped that old tradition some time ago and gave up running School House. "What on earth are you going to do?" one Housemaster asked him... The best reply, possibly applicable only to the Head about whom it was said, came from a master at Eton last term to the question from a bemused new boy "What on earth does the Headmaster do?" "What doesn't he do?" was the response.

The same applies to Houseparents and that is why it seems appropriate to finish on a note of resonance even if the context is one of captivity. Two teenage cowboys are in prison in Mexico in Cormac McCarthy's fine novel (the first of 'The Border Trilogy') *all the pretty horses*. One of them dreams of the horses he loves. You may think that the lack of punctuation has done away with self-discipline; it has not and what beauty and praise there is:

> *That night he dreamt of horses in a field on a high plain where the spring rains had brought up the grass and the wildflowers out of the ground and the flowers ran all blue and yellow far as the eye could see and in the dream he was among the horses running and in the dream he himself could run with the horses and they coursed the young mares and fillies over the plain where their rich bay and their rich chestnut colors shone in the sun and the young*

colts ran with their dams and trampled down the flowers in a haze of pollen that hung in the sun like powdered gold and they ran he and the horses out along the high mesas where the ground resounded under their running hooves and they flowed and changed and ran and their manes and tails blew off them like spume and there was nothing else at all in that high world and they moved all of them in a resonance that was like a music among them and they were none of them afraid horse nor colt nor mare and they ran in that resonance which is the world itself and which cannot be spoken but only praised.

So Housemasters and Housemistresses are men and women who make peace out of war and who try to plant that productive outlook in their charges. You will remember only too well, and I am still writing this at a time of remembrance, the lines from Micah that refer to strong nations beating their swords into ploughshares and their spears into pruning hooks but I hope that you can find a place in your hearts for the verse that follows. It is one for which all of us who have our homes in Houses or in Schools yearn and for which we work together: '*but they shall sit every man under his vine and under his fig tree; and none shall make them afraid.*'

Michael Mavor was a boarder at Loretto, Headmaster of Gordonstoun from 1979 - 1990, and since then has been Head Master of Rugby School. He was Chairman of HMC in 1997.

Chapter 11

Marketing Boarding

by Edward Gould

Master, Marlborough College

Amongst the ever increasing quantity of junk mail that passes across a Head's desk on a daily basis, there lies quite frequently a pamphlet enticing the Head to use the services of a marketing organisation or consultant. Your problems will be solved, you are told, with the use of various marketing tools, a new prospectus, a video, the creation and maintenance of a website, a CD Rom and the eternal money spinner for the consultant, a PR campaign promoting your school.

The temptation to go down one of these routes when there is difficulty recruiting boarders and a perceived or real pressure from governing bodies is considerable. Of course, there are very few who would deny the need for an up to date prospectus and, given the range of boarding offers across the independent sector, many Heads or perhaps some Governors or Development Officers, more familiar with the world of commerce, may believe other marketing tools to be beneficial as well.

It is not easy to ensure their success but breaking down the barriers to entry to boarding schools is an important need and there is much truth in the statement that a school's and house's fate is sealed by conversation around the dinner tables of those able to consider sending their children to our schools. Communication, therefore, is central to marketing and the debate arguably should focus on the nature and content of that communication and less on the means of communication.

At this stage it must be said that I have no formal marketing qualifications and the thoughts that follow are derived from experience, together with research conducted by the Boarding Education Alliance. It is recognised that within the boarding sector, the range of schools is wide and clearly policies which suit one category of school will not necessarily suit another. Houseparents, however, play a vital role in the marketing of a school.

It has been fashionable in some quarters to attack the concept of a boarding education and it is undeniable that the number of boarders in ISC schools has fallen. Certainly the reduction in overseas service postings has provided a shrinking pool of custom and more recently the financial crisis affecting the economies in the Far East has not helped. The recession at the start of the 1990s did little to help either and the present level of fees and the upward trend above annual levels of inflation should concern us all; but now the economy is strong and throughout the difficulties, the demand for independent education has remained strong. Boarding is not for all children but there are many more out there for whom modern boarding is appropriate. The marketing of boarding needs to respond to modern family life and boarding has to prove itself as a kind of investment by offering to equip children for the future society that they will inhabit.

The boarding sector has been slow to adjust to modern social trends identified by the Henley Centre and because there has been no sustained marketing in the independent boarding sector until recently, schools and houses tend to promote themselves (their own brand identity) rather than the advantages of boarding. Equally fee information is slipped in as an insert to the prospectus and with no reference to value for money. Promotional imagery and language, too, is frequently directed at those with a predisposition to buy. Is there sufficient attention paid to combating the outmoded perceptions of boarding often reinforced by the media – Dickensian environment, education for the Upper Classes, the old school tie, club or elite? In our promotion, do we aim at the non-traditional parent or do we reinforce traditional activities such as the CCF and Chapel or school ancestry, gowns, *etc*, all of which are potentially negative images to the non-traditional parent of today? Schools are not exempt either from the current trend in society to denigrate traditional authorities, which command increasingly less respect. The size of boarding's commercial opportunity is a function of how radically we are prepared to adjust to social change and how successfully we can highlight its real, as opposed to its traditional, benefits to special types of parents.

Much of the received wisdom today points towards family disintegration, the increasing divorce rate, the rising number of single parents and partners setting up home together. This has led to the quick response by some that boarding is for those in need and those perceived as being in an abnormal situation: those whose parents live abroad or in remote locations; those from single families; those in need of special help. This imagery invokes a defensive position and engenders a feeling of 'this is not for the likes of us' from families who feel they have no special need. Good boarding schools may well help these children but they do so simply because the majority of the school is made up of children from united and loving families, who rather than neglecting their responsibilities, have taken the decision to give their children the widest opportunities. They form an active partnership with their chosen schools and houses. Indeed to take this decision parents need to have appreciated their position honestly, to have shown courage and to know that the family bonds of love and respect are strong and secure.

A report by the Future Foundation highlighted a number of strands, which need to be appreciated when marketing is considered. Rather than family disintegration, the report tells us that family structures have strengthened across this generation. No longer do they hold excessive nostalgia for earlier times and the good old days. Parents are now spending more time with their children and many are taking a much more ordered, more professional, yet just as loving, approach to parenting in all its varied responsibilities.

However, some 60% of working couples with children confirm the presence of serious time pressures in their lives. In professional, dual income families, now more commonplace, these time pressures shape much of the family culture. Meals are less frequently taken together and these parents have little time to expand their children's horizons, for example. Greater affluence means that they can afford boarding. To meet this demand, a variety of boarding offers from full boarding through weekly boarding to other short term arrangements have developed in recent years. Yet no parent wants their child to stand out like a sore thumb within a community. Part of the idea of security lies in there being other children experiencing the same education and there is a need for schools to identify carefully the type of boarding opportunity they wish to offer.

Parents want a blend balanced according to the demands on their lives between seeing their children, being able to communicate through e-mail, mobile phones, fax machines and pagers and yet knowing that their children are safe and being exposed to opportunities which can be provided only by boarding. Schools cannot insulate themselves from the communications culture of our times. The feeling of guilt that our opponents like to promote in parents considering boarding will not be allayed by defensive posturing towards modern aids in communication.

Whether internet facilities are needed for advertising is debatable, but they are needed to enable families to communicate effectively. Maybe the next decade will see video links universally installed in schools to contribute further to the 'death of distance' within human contact. Whatever measures are put in place, children are nevertheless absent from parents and the role of Houseparents remains central to successful communication during a boarding education. Surprise is sometimes expressed that Housemasters or Housemistresses are in the majority of cases family people themselves and that these families have every interest in sustaining open communication with parents. Stressing this in marketing helps break down barriers that many parents and prospective parents perceive. These parents need prompt responses and it needs to be stated that modern boarding is not about one way communication between the remote institution and the anxious parent but rather a two-way flow between two sets of families, 'House' and 'home'.

Increasingly parents have an 'anxiety agenda' that concerns threats to their children's welfare. They want specific answers to questions about drugs, smoking, bullying, security, eating disorders, sexual behaviour and all manner of problems. The Children Act and subsequent inspections have done much to reassure yet, in marketing schools and houses successfully, there needs to be an uninhibited dialogue with parents and their children about all today's temptations. Clear and well supported policies, even if the word is dreaded, are needed. We cannot insulate children from all evils but boarding does provide a significant degree of security: a safe place in which children can learn from their mistakes.

The report also focussed on two further points: the diversity of the nature of the family unit and the increasing democracy found in families. It makes clear that there is no prototype family in our secular, multi-cultural society today. In the decision-making process concerning the choice of school, children have a far greater influence. Boarding schools contain a section of the normal population, which is a point not readily appreciated by all prospective parents. Inevitably schools come into contact with all the joys and difficulties life brings. Prospective parents need reassurance that boarding is 'for the likes of us'. They are concerned that they may be placing their child in an environment and community, which will bring further pressures to an already over-pressurised life, and new entrants worry about 'elitism'. No school offers elitism; rather good boarding schools are specialist schools with vast experience of looking after adolescents. The young need equal reassurance on these points and it follows that the children need as much attention as parents on Open days and visits if marketing is to be successful. Academic constraints there may be on entry but in other respects, the normality of other children and families within today's social trends needs stressing.

Within the characteristics of the modern family, the Henley Centre research identified six Parent Groups with differing attitudes to boarding.

> First there are the Ideologues. This group is opposed to boarding in principle or because of a political or quasi-moral stance. They object to private education rather than boarding as such and accusations of elitism abound with fees being the mechanism by which it is maintained.

> Then there are the disgruntled former boarders. This group experienced boarding and did not enjoy it. They felt the experience had been 'damaging', did not see a 'good reason' for being 'sent away'. The common denominator of this group is that they were all under 11 when they first boarded.

Regular e-mail contact with home is essential.

Thirdly, the attached parents – this group is anxious about sending children away to school either because selfishly they will miss them or because they fear their children will grow away from them. The feelings of guilt on the part of these parents are strong.

A further group of parents was classified as "Double income in-a-hurry". This group is founded on recent social change. It is made up of some former boarders and those who can afford it since both parents are working. The benefits of boarding need to be made compelling and value-for-money issues will be raised.

What about "Nervous new money"? This group has not considered boarding and because of outmoded perceptions had thought it not for them. They can see the advantages but need to be assured that modern boarding is for them.

Finally, there are the traditional boarders. This group consists of former boarders who enjoyed the experience and they will seek a boarding education for their children. The choice of school will be determined by what they read, see and hear.

While the Henley Centre Report includes approaches that can be adopted towards each group, the thrust of the marketing message is that if the approach to the 'double income in-a-hurry' and 'Nervous new money' groups is perfected, the right kind of messages will be going to the 'Attached parents' and 'Disgruntled former boarders' groups. The 'Traditional boarders' will enter the market anyway and the 'Ideologues' will never buy in.

Awareness of family lifestyles, current social trends, anxiety about children and the attitudes of parent groups may help to direct marketing but it fails to identify the niche of a boarding education.

When asked the question 'why boarding?', Heads and Houseparents will doubtless respond with a familiar list of points: a wider range of opportunities, better use being made of time, learning self-reliance, learning new experiences and how to handle success and disappointment within a safe environment.

However, boarding offers more than this and here I must acknowledge the help of Ted Maidment, Headmaster of Shrewsbury. Boarding schools set out to do so much more than day schools. More questions are raised and more problems are faced. The challenges are greater, for boarding schools are communities living together and, as a result, all issues have to be addressed, they cannot be sidelined or brushed under the carpet. Neither are 40 minute PSHE lessons the answer. They are in a boarding school the centre of every day life. Much of this case for boarding revolves around the merits of living in a total community. The feel, colour, richness and drama of life provide an undeniable quality.

Yet these communities consist of individuals on whom much individual care is lavished. Parents appreciate the deep and detailed knowledge that Houseparents have of their children as a result of their professionalism and the total resources available for their children. The individuals, not personalities, learn their strengths and weaknesses without hopefully arrogance or shame of either respectively and, through living in the community, the young gain a tolerance, respect and consideration for others to a degree far beyond that provided in a day school. The genuine power of friendship is more strongly forged, too, through shared experiences. This should not be dismissed as the embryonic 'old school tie' culture for our school communities provide plenty of opportunities where individuals can make their own decisions over a range of issues, including friendships, and they necessarily have to learn to live with the consequences of those decisions. A boarding school with its 24 hour day can achieve so much more than a day school in the interests of individual development for each individual child.

Much of this is probably best left for conversation with prospective parents who come to us with an open mind and a strong feeling that a good boarding education may be hugely beneficial to their family. The seeds can nevertheless be sown in marketing literature.

When the next marketing consultant's flier arrives on your desk, it may be the answer to your prayers. But before returning the reply paid card, it might be helpful to consider a few questions first. Do you want the services of the consultant or do you really need to conduct market research? Why did those pupils chose another school or House when registered for you? What do your parents think? What area(s) can you try to enter in this country before looking overseas? Is your boarding offer clear? Does your literature portray your school as a specialist school likely to meet the need of today's families or is it resting on past achievements? Are Houseparents giving out the right messages for today? How useful is your advertising and is it cost effective? Are there barriers to entry that need to be lifted? Do your feeder schools really know what is happening? The list could go on. In general we are coy as a sector in recognising openly that we are in the selling game: Schools and Houses have to sell their boarding offer. Thinking carefully about the process through which prospective parents and their children pass may well prove more significant than adopting the latest marketing gimmick. Between 2000 and 2005 the cohort of children aged 11-15 and 16-18 increases by 1.5% and 7.1%

respectively, the economy is strong and there are many who believe a good boarding education to be the best education. At around £60 or less a day at 2000 prices it is good value!

*Edward Gould was a boarder at St Edward's School, Oxford.
He was Housemaster of the Headmaster's House, Harrow and became
Headmaster of Felsted School in 1983.
Since 1993 he has been Master of Marlborough College.
He was also Chairman of the Boarding education Alliance.*

Chapter 12

The Financial Perspective

by Vivian Anthony

Secretary of HMC

No other country in the world has such a high proportion of school pupils in boarding schools. Even the dramatic decline in the overall number of boarders in Britain has not changed that position. Indeed Britain is not alone in experiencing a decline: schools in Australia, United States and Canada are among those reporting falling boarding numbers. The tradition of boarding, as an educational experience, has been principally a feature of independent schools in the English Speaking world. However with the growth of independent schools in Eastern Europe and the Far East pupils have been living away from home but usually in hostels rather than boarding houses. Some of the East European students who have won scholarships to study in HMC schools have come from highly selective schools in their own country. In some cases these schools are far from their homes and lack of suitable transport arrangements makes it impossible for them to live at home. They think nothing of looking after themselves in a hostel from the age of thirteen. Pupils from Africa and China tell similar stories; but this is not the British tradition. While some pupils board because there would be no other sensible way of attending the school of their choice, most are at boarding schools because they and their parents see it as a valuable experience which enhances their education.

There are of course a wide variety of boarding experiences on offer. The major boarding schools, where a high proportion of the pupils are boarders and the fees are at the top end of the scale, provide a different service from those schools where boarders are in the minority and fees are lower. In the main, in education as in other things, you get what you pay for. Schools charging high fees can offer a lot more in the way of facilities. However, many low fee schools offer excellent value for money and in the matter of academic results, where other factors come into play, they can hold their own remarkably well. Parents are, quite rightly, looking for more than simply good academic results. They believe that while good results win places at good universities, and this is a high priority, other qualities are important in determining who will be successful later in life. They hope that boarding will help to develop those qualities.

Some independent schools are more successful than others and the reasons for their success extend far beyond their boarding facilities. There is a virtuous circle: success breeds success; more pupils apply and the school becomes more selective; good teachers are attracted and results improve further. Competition for places enables the school to raise fees and the additional income can be used to improve facilities and offer more scholarships and bursaries to clever pupils. There is also a vicious circle: schools go into a downward spiral leading, in some cases, to closure.

It is interesting to explore how economic factors influence the success of boarding schools. In a market with declining numbers the ability to attract new families into boarding is vital. In fact a significant proportion of those taking up boarding places today are first time buyers. The parents, who traditionally sent their children to boarding schools, have been succeeded by a new generation in different circumstances. Those who work and live abroad turn to local schools providing a 'British Style' education. Some of these schools are in overseas membership of HMC. Travel has become so much easier that even those working a long way from home choose to leave wife and family at home and return at weekends: often the children will be day pupils. The armed services have heavily pruned their numbers and opportunities for overseas postings are much reduced. Some lower-fee boarding schools depend greatly on this clientele and are now suffering the consequences.

The increase in overseas business postings has barely compensated for the decline in those in the diplomatic service. While many commercial firms are willing to give support for the education of the children of those they send overseas this has not been enough to persuade some parents of the merits of boarding education. However schools are working hard to attract the children of expatriate parents and the number of children from overseas is steadily increasing, though most of these are from foreign families. This success, and the possibility of further expansion in this market, will be analysed elsewhere.

Attracting new families into boarding requires great skills. While skilful presentation is part of this, the new breed of parents want to 'feel the cloth' and appreciate the full quality of boarding experience. Parents have come to expect high standards. Visits to schools and to boarding houses are a regular part of my job. Whether as HMC Secretary on special occasions, as an inspector or as a governor, there have been many opportunities to observe the variety of the product. At one end of the spectrum the quality of the accommodation is at least as good as that of most university halls of residence. In these schools all the Sixth Form and Year 11 pupils are in single study bedrooms. Where there has been new building or extensive renovation, these rooms will have en-suite bathroom facilities. Even the junior pupils will have single studies though they will share bedrooms or dormitories in twos or threes. The bedroom and study furniture will be modern and of good quality. Each study in the House will be wired for linking into the school's Intranet or the wider Internet, and computers will be available for those who do not have their own.

Contrast this with the scenario at the low fee end of the market. All but a few chosen pupils in their final year will be in dormitories and shared studies. The furniture will be old and damaged. The washing facilities will be communal and the showers may not be as clean as they should be, with green mould and other evidence of damp on the walls. Dirty linen is strewn about and little effort will have been made to tidy studies or dormitories. The pupils may not notice, or may even like it, but mothers will not approve and they will move on to the next school.

Accommodation and furniture are of course not the most important aspects of boarding education but they have the most immediate impact on the potential parent. If first impressions are not right they may not stay to discover that the house has a caring regime and a range of activities to rank with the best. It will need superhuman efforts by the Houseparent, tutors and prefects to win back the disillusioned visitors. There is however a Catch 22 in all this: to arrest the decline in boarding numbers there must be high investment in accommodation and facilities; but who will want to invest, or be able to find the funds, if boarding numbers are in decline?

Most boarding schools have Houses dating back to Victorian times and, while they may be externally attractive, they are hopelessly uneconomic to run, difficult to adapt to meet modern demands and rather gloomy and forbidding inside. Small fortunes can be spent in less than successful attempts to bring them up to date, though there are honourable exceptions to this rule. Many schools have spent millions of pounds upgrading while others have built state of the art new boarding Houses for rather less. What is more, the result is a House which is easy and cheap to run, and to maintain. Such new Houses are usually built with holiday lettings in mind, adding to their profitability.

We have seen that these investment decisions are not easy for schools facing a decline in numbers. Do nothing and the numbers will fall faster. Spend heavily and you may be throwing good money after bad. Unlike some aspects of education it is not easy to vary costs in boarding. It is a high fixed cost scenario. The House must be built and maintained. There must be a Houseparent to run it with the tutors and the residents must have their own suitable accommodation. The other house staff, including matrons, cooks, cleaners and handymen, must be employed and the heating and other running costs must be found. Hardly any of these costs fall if there are fewer boarders. There will be a budget break-even point and if the number of boarders falls below that the house will be running at a loss. Moreover there is little that can be done about it because these costs are largely fixed. If this position continues the school will be forced to close the House or perhaps amalgamate Houses. Other strategies have been tried and sometimes with success. Schools have become coeducational and turned a failing boys' House into a thriving girls' House. Some have extended the age range of the school below 13. However, boarding has been in greater difficulties in the lower age range. Others have turned to the foreign market, but sometimes this has also been fraught with difficulties.

There is another picture. Some schools have turned round a failing boarding situation by bravely investing in new facilities. As boarders returned to the school the breakeven point was crossed and each boarder above that number added greatly to the surplus earned by the House. Apart from wear and tear and a few consumables costs do not rise as the extra places are filled and the income is increased. There are dangers in packing too many into a House. Well designed and furnished dormitories can be spoilt by adding extra beds. However if spaces can be found for a few more boarders then the additional funds they generate can be made available for further investment. Mixed day/boarding schools usually find boarding places are the more profitable. Although not easy to achieve, it is worth striving for flexibility of accommodation. When building for boarding the architect should consider possible alternative uses for the building if boarding numbers are not maintained. Some boarding Houses have been successfully converted into Sixth Form centres. One school is planning a building, off-campus, which could be converted into an old peoples' home!

The quality of life within a House depends heavily on the skill and dedication of the Houseparent and the tutors and there are costs associated with this. Good but cheap boarding is almost a contradiction in terms. Running a boarding House requires a high level of dedication and some sacrifices on the part of the family. While they are usually and properly provided with good accommodation, there is a sense in which their 'home' is not really theirs, and not simply in ownership terms. Members of the boarding house will be regularly invited to informal social occasions apart from the many times they will be in the study to discuss their progress or their problems. In some ways the position of resident house tutor is even more domestically demanding if their accommodation is in the middle of the

The resident tutor has many roles, including House banker.

House. Salaries and conditions must be sufficiently attractive to persuade the best teachers to take on this crucial and rewarding role. The tradition in some schools of employing non-teachers as Houseparents is understandable but it misses out on the advantage of having someone in charge of the pupils who has a good view of the whole picture in and out of class. The same is true of the other House positions and particularly those of matron and cook, where there is still feeding in House. Too many schools have been willing to employ refugees from society in these important jobs. A good matron can take many problems off the shoulders of the Houseparent and spouse. She must be given the conditions to do the job properly. Many matrons say that they are assigned those corners of the House for which no other purpose can be found. First time boarding families have high expectations. They expect a good deal of the Houseparent's time; flexible arrangements, so that they can see their children when they want to; a high standard of care; instant attention to bullying and other problems; and a good understanding of their children on the part of all who come across them. To deal with such pressures the boarding House must be well staffed, with enough non-resident tutors to spread the load. It is on account of these extra duties that boarding schools have extra staffing and higher salary scales. This is just one of the aspects of the financial affairs of boarding schools which must be considered.

While each school's accounts are unique there are enough common features to make analysis and benchmarking worthwhile. Various firms of auditors, like MacIntyre, Price Waterhouse Coopers and Kidson, publish regular surveys. In broad percentage terms, Expenditure in Senior Boarding Schools is allocated to Teaching 40%, Academic expenses 5%, and Activities 2%; Administrative and Support Costs 11% [including 6% on staff]; Building & Grounds 21% [including nearly 10% on staff]; Boarding/Welfare Costs ie maintenance, medical, catering 22% [including 13% on staff]. As each school treats these items differently accounts have to be examined carefully before comparisons can be made. For example, one boarding school has a benchmark of 30% for the expenditure on teachers' salaries but accounts separately for those elements which can be assigned to running boarding houses or school administration, ie Houseparents and Head.

As the proportion of day pupils increases so the percentage spent on boarding/welfare and building and grounds decreases and the percentage spent on teaching, academic and activities costs increases. These are of courses percentages and not actual amounts. Teacher:pupil ratios are more favourable for boarding schools, currently around 1:7 compared with day/boarding 1:9 and for all HMC schools 1:10.5. In 2000 there are fewer than 20 HMC schools and about 40 independent schools which have more than 90% of their pupils boarding. On the other hand there are fewer than 90 schools which have no boarders. Smaller schools spend a higher proportion on salaries than larger schools because of economies of scale. The salary and benefits for a Houseparent are not related to the number of boarders in his House. In the USA where the Houses, or dorms as they are called, can be very small, a Houseparent may be responsible for more than one 'House'.

Boarding schools usually have different salary scales from those of day/boarding schools though, once again, each school is different. Boarding schools have long spines of 30 or more points and many do not apply bars to progress up the scale. Houseparents are sometimes rewarded with a specific allowance, which is relinquished at the end of the post; others are accelerated up the main scale. Schools with more day pupils have scales, which are closer to the national pay scales, in which progress beyond the short basic scale depends on extra responsibilities. However the introduction of Performance Related Pay for good teachers may affect these arrangements. Average teacher salaries in boarding schools were around £31,000 in 2000, with the highest paid teachers receiving nearly £40,000. In day/boarding the average was around £26,000 and scales seldom exceed £33,000.

Average salaries are higher in boys' schools where, as in boarding schools, teachers are paid for extra duties. Larger schools also tend to pay higher salaries. In recent years increases in the costs of employing teachers have been rising faster than fee income and these pressures are unlikely to diminish. Moreover unit costs have been rising as pupil numbers fall, class sizes and class contact time are reduced. These trends in unit costs will have to be addressed if boarding is to flourish. Is there a good reason why class sizes should be smaller in boarding schools than in day schools? Examination results do not suggest that schools with small classes are more successful. Teacher cost per pupil is higher in a small school (c£3,500) than in a large school (c£2,900), and it is higher in a boarding school (c£5,000) than in day/boarding (c£ 3,700).

Welfare costs show similar variation between size and type of school. The more pupils over whom the medical, pastoral and catering costs can be spread the lower the unit costs. Schools have to choose between the cost savings of contracted out central catering and the in-house catering favoured by many parents for the atmosphere it creates. This favourable atmosphere may cost 15-20% more.

Differences in unit costs also occur in the maintenance of buildings and grounds, traditionally boarding schools have needed more playing fields to provide the expected wide range of activities and of course they have more buildings. Costs per pupil are c£3,000 compared with c£2,000 in day/boarding and less than £1,000 in HMC day schools. Huge amounts have been spent on new buildings and equipment in recent years, though the difference between successful and less successful schools is considerable. The Year 2000 ISIS census shows that over £80 million was spent by HMC schools on new buildings in the previous year and nearly £70 million on improvements to buildings and equipment. It is interesting to know what proportion of this was spent on boarding accommodation and facilities. Some governing bodies have been reluctant to spend on boarding unless they were confident of a good return. It is not easy to justify a loan of say £2 million for boarding improvements if numbers are in decline. The recent ISIS survey shows that about £50 million a year is being spent by boarding schools to build and improve boarding facilities. The 1999 ISIS survey, to which nearly half of the 600 boarding schools responded, indicated that in the previous two years, 154 schools had spent £63.7 million on major developments, and 124 planned to spend £55.3 million in the following two years.

Fee concessions are under discussion in all schools. The proportion of gross income going on this item has been rising. ISIS commented 'the increasing number of pupils receiving help with their fees has been a long-term trend; it accelerated during the 1990s recession as more families needed bursaries to enable children at crucial examination stages to complete their courses.' 30% of children receive help with their fees compared with around 15% in 1982, when the census first began. These concessions are varied: scholarships, bursaries, fee reductions for the children of staff and former pupils, children of clergy, armed services, doctors, and reductions for second and subsequent children at the school. Scholarships are awarded to children who show ability in one or more areas - academic, music, art, sport, 'all-rounder', *etc.* Bursaries are awarded to applicants who meet the standard of entry to the school but are unable to afford full fees.

While it is a main objective of most schools to make it possible for children from poorer homes to enjoy the benefits of the education it provides, there is a concern that concessions on fees are used to attract pupils who might otherwise go to other schools. Discounting of fees is against the code of practice for independent schools and is said to occur in private 'under the counter' deals between unscrupulous heads and parents, who are willing to trade around for the best deal. For the individual school, which is unable to fill empty places, such deals are attractive if they cover at least the marginal cost of educating the pupil. However at a macro-level they drive down net fee levels particularly among those schools which are effectively 'recruiters' rather than 'selectors'. It is a dangerous spiral as when parents become aware of the existence of discounts, they are often unwilling to pay the full fee.

On average schools are giving concessions of 6% of gross fee income. However this figure includes the shortfall from the Assisted Places income, which results from fee-capping. It does not include the cost of awards which are funded from other sources *eg* endowment or trust income, and for a few schools this is considerable. There are schools, which allocate to concessions more than 10% of fee income, while others provide little more than the 2% required of them by the Charity Commissioners. With the demise of the Assisted Places Scheme schools have to find more money for bursaries from their own resources and they are responding well to the challenge. Last year a further 8% of pupils were given assistance. Schools are searching for other sources of funding for this purpose and Peter Lampl and Peter Ogden are among those who made substantial contributions. Following the amazing success of the fundraising industry in the USA, HMC schools are setting up Development Offices to try the same approach. High among their goals will be funding for assisting less advantaged pupils. In the most successful US schools less than 50% of their income comes from fees and a much higher proportion than in the UK goes on fee concessions. Advice on the optimum proportion is impossible because so much depends on the particular circumstances of the school. Surveys suggest that schools currently giving the highest proportion are smaller, day/boarding and coeducational.

In 1991 the National Association of Independent Schools, the largest such organisation in the world and based in the USA, set up a Project on Pricing and Affordability. There is a concern that school fees are going up so rapidly that schools are pricing themselves out of the market. A glance at the chart produced each year by ISIS shows that in almost every year fee increases have outstripped not only the RPI but also average earnings in Britain. While it could be argued that the more relevant comparison would be with the earnings of those families willing to consider boarding education it remains a fact that boarding numbers are falling. Surveys for explanations of why potential parents do not choose boarding list changing social attitudes but some schools say that parents invent these arguments to cover the fact that they simply cannot afford the fees. At over £16,000 per annum for one child, to be found out of taxed income, that sounds plausible. However, the wealthy have been getting wealthier and the gap between them and the average independent school parent has been getting wider. This may explain why the top boarding schools appear to be attracting good numbers of applicants while others are struggling. The demand for places does not appear to be price sensitive, at least as far as existing parents are concerned, but with each significant rise potential parents seem to transfer their allegiance to the day market.

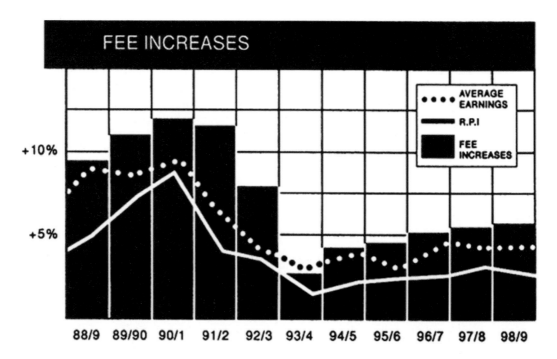

The graph illustrates fee rises since 1988-89 against the background of the RPI and average earnings over the same period. Historically, teachers' salaries have often outpaced or matched the RPI through national awards alone, without taking incremental rises into account. [ISIS Annual Census 1999, p 3]

Among the conclusions of the NAIS project was the need for further research. 'It is clear that high tuitions [fees] limit, or at least significantly define, who attends them. But most of the questions that are most important to schools – how to market themselves, how to target the markets, how to expand their markets, how to differentiate the market, how to subsidise one portion of the market and not the other – cannot be answered without knowing something about the socio-economic characteristics' of potential families not using the schools. 'Family income information for all families using [boarding] schools, and other information that differentiates these families from those choosing other schools is critical to marketing, to targeting, and to policy impact analysis.'

A research project entitled *The UK Market for Boarding Education in the 1990s* was carried out by Karl Spencer and Michael Hay of the London Business School and the findings were used to inform the activities of the Boarding Education Alliance. The analysis pointed out that the success of independent schools in general and boarding schools in particular depends upon the health of the economy. Working at the time of the recession of the early 1990s they were rightly pessimistic about the short term situation. This pessimism was not dispelled by Heads who expected further reductions in numbers. Their belief that the rate of decline will be slowed by the up-turn of the economy, by improved marketing and by seeking other forms of revenue and new-breed customers, is also proving to be correct.

There is a continuing role for boarding schools in the third millennium but only if schools address with confidence the right issues and effect sensible strategies. The day of the colourful amateur is over: schools will need to be highly professional in their approach and to make use of the services of the best experts they can find.

Vivian Anthony is Secretary of the HMC. He ran a house at Tonbridge School and was Headmaster of Colfe's School from 1976 - 1990.

Chapter 13

Inspection of Boarding

by Dr Roger Morgan

Chief Inspector, Oxfordshire County Council

Under the Children Act of 1989, those looking after pupils aged under 18 in independent boarding schools have a legal duty to 'safeguard and promote' their welfare. Under the new Care Standards Act 2000, this duty will extend to every boarding school, including LEA schools and non-maintained special schools, and to Further Education colleges. How well schools fulfil this welfare duty towards boarders is inspected under the Children Act, quite separately from inspections of academic provision undertaken by OfSTED. Boarding provision is however also included as one of the many aspects of the operation of a boarding school during wider ISI or OfSTED inspections. Separate welfare inspections are currently carried out by local social services departments; in 2002 the government plans to transfer responsibility for all welfare inspections to the new National Commission for Care Standards (and to the National Assembly in Wales).

You will no doubt hear many stories about what you are and are not allowed to do under the Children Act (even from some of your pupils!). The Children Act does not in fact go beyond requiring you and the school to safeguard and promote the welfare of each individual child (pupil under 18) you accommodate. The law does not set out any list of politically correct 'do's' and 'don'ts'. The government produces guidance about sound welfare practice in schools, on which inspectors base their inspections. The main document is Volume 5 of the Children Act Guidance and Regulations series, published by the Stationery Office. This was amended by a government circular from the Department of Health in 1995, known as Local Authority Circular (LAC) 95(1), also obtainable from the Stationery Office. These documents are vital if you are planning major changes to welfare arrangements in your school or house, if you are involved in a dispute about a welfare issue – or if a welfare inspection is imminent!

The first major question is what really constitutes good welfare practice on any wet Monday at school. A few guiding principles are important. First, the law requires you to 'safeguard' welfare – this means having the systems in place, and the atmosphere and practice in the house, to protect your pupils from harm such as significant bullying, physical risks to their health and safety, and from abuse by either adults or other pupils. Secondly, the legal requirement to 'promote' welfare means that you have a duty to provide a positive welfare service, alongside the school's academic provisions. Thirdly, the law gives you a welfare duty to each individual pupil, not only the 'pupil body' as a whole, and you are required to promote the welfare of even those pupils who do not fit in to the school or house, who perhaps were placed in the wrong school altogether, and even those who are about to be expelled. Finally, the term 'accommodation' does not only mean physically within the house on the school site; the school's welfare duty extends to all boarders even when they are outside the house or the school – in town, staying with friends or guardians (if the school rather than their own parents arranged that accommodation for them), while travelling under school-made arrangements, and when staying away on activities (including school arranged accommodation abroad and activities run for the school by other organisations, such as CCF camps and exercises and licensed adventure centres).

A set of National Boarding Standards has been written in preparation for the transfer of welfare inspections to the National Commission. These will then replace the different local standards currently used by social services. For the first time, these standards and criteria will apply to all boarders in all types of school throughout the country, and will be the yardstick against which inspectors will inspect and report on your welfare arrangements. These standards have been developed through the National Boarding Standards Committee for submission to the government for their final decision on adoption for use by the National Commission. The have been developed from existing best practice, jointly by the schools' Associations, existing inspectorates and government departments. They represent minimum standards, not requirements either to spend excessive money nor to achieve the unrealistic.

The new National Standards serve well to define what is meant by good welfare practice in boarding. They cover the policies and systems that need to be in place to safeguard and promote boarders' welfare, the physical requirements of boarding houses and other forms of accommodation (including the lodgings used by some schools and sixth form colleges, together with off site 'field' accommodation and camps), staffing requirements, and everyday good practice issues. In short, they cover policies, premises and people. The standards themselves are increasingly recognised as reasonable, appropriate and attainable amongst schools as well as by inspectors and government officials, and there is a remarkable degree of consistency of view between these different interests.

Current government guidance requires full welfare inspections of independent boarding schools every four years, with informal contacts (such as brief follow up visits or contact calls) between these. Government guidance requires some schools to be inspected more frequently, usually with a full inspection every two years. These include schools without governing bodies, schools with significant numbers of pupils having statements of special educational needs or who rarely have contact with their parents, schools which are not members of Associations such as HMC, and schools where there have recently been significant welfare concerns.

Inspectors may make an extra visit to follow up particular recommendations or even to give advice – schools can and do ask for advice from their inspectorate on issues such as the design of adaptations or new build boarding accommodation, or on dealing with a tricky welfare issue. Different inspectorates (such as those inspecting welfare and those primarily inspecting academic arrangements) are required to cooperate to space their inspections out, to avoid placing excessive demands on schools by carrying out different inspections too close together.

The law gives specific rights to inspectors. They are entitled to enter the school, to meet and question pupils, and to inspect premises, school or house records (including those kept on a computer) that include welfare or health information about boarders (the latter relating to school, rather than NHS, records). They can visit unannounced, without making a prior appointment. They can interview staff and inspect staff personnel records (usually to check upon staff recruitment procedures). Welfare inspectors can visit classrooms if they wish. It is an offence to obstruct an inspector carrying out their lawful inspection functions in the school or house. However, you have a right to demand that any inspector proves their identity before entering or inspecting anything – by law an inspector under the Children Act must carry identification, and must on demand show a further document authorising them to inspect your school. Since the law requires them to carry these documents, you should always ask inspectors to show these on arrival, and should not hesitate to deny entry or access to pupils if you are not shown these documents.

In the past, each local social services authority has been expected to determine how to meet its inspection duties, resulting in different inspection processes in different areas. Most inspections involve two inspectors, but in many areas you can expect one inspector working alone, and in some, a team of inspectors. Welfare inspections typically involve smaller teams than OfSTED, ISI or school Association inspections. Do not however make the mistake of treating the findings of a smaller scale and locally based welfare inspection more lightly than a much larger scale wider school inspection – both can have a similar impact on the school and its future.

Before a welfare inspection, the school is likely to be consulted over the inspection programme, inspectors unfamiliar with the school may make an informal acquaintance visit before arriving on the inspection proper, and the school is likely to be asked to fill in a pre-inspection questionnaire about its welfare systems and to provide copies of key documents.

The inspection is likely to take place over a number of days, involving a number of inspection activities. The inspection process will become standardised nationally with the future establishment of the National Commission (many schools were involved with inspectors in piloting a standardised inspection methodology to accompany the draft National Boarding Standards).

Most inspections will involve individual interviews with key staff, including the Head, and where applicable, Head of boarding, Houseparents, Matron or Sister, Chaplain, School Doctor, School Counsellor, Bursar, Health and Safety Officer, and child protection liaison officer. Group discussions may be held with staff, such as house teams, tutors, matrons, activity staff, or gap students. In such discussions, inspectors will be gathering information needed to assess the school against welfare standards. They will aim to corroborate information from different sources (such as records, information from staff, information from pupils, and their own observations). The best policy in responding is therefore to be honest and factual, and the best preparation is to get hold of a copy of the standards to be used so that you know what the inspectors are assessing. Any boarding school with different houses can be expected to have major differences between houses in both atmosphere and practice, so be ready to explain these.

Inspectors will also speak to pupils during their inspection, both informally as they observe what is going on around the school, in the house in the morning and during the evening, and as they visit activities, or dine with pupils. They may wish to meet selected groups of pupils, from different years or houses, from a minority group within the school, or prefects, new boarders, or pupils who have recently been accommodated in off site locations. Inspectors will often ask to be shown around each house by pupils from the house, to assess the premises and learn the pupils' view of how the house works. Be prepared for inspectors to select pupils at random for such activities – this helps to secure a cross section of pupil views, and avoids ending up mainly hearing from the school's inevitable 'barrack room lawyers'! If any pupil selected in this way does not want to be involved, tell the inspector – they should respect this and invite another pupil.

Many welfare inspections involve a pupil survey. Many staff feel concerned at this, worrying that certain pupils will take the opportunity either to make mischief or to wreak revenge for some recent perceived wrong. Certainly ask how the inspectors intend to interpret the results, what they will do if pupils make allegations against named staff or other pupils (although note that pupils may do this otherwise than through a survey, and inspectors would be looking for corroborative evidence of anything they are going to take seriously), certainly ask to see a copy of the survey form before it is used – and discuss anything you are concerned about.

Surveys are a standard tool to secure people's views in many contexts, and can provide vital information on the 'state of the welfare nation' at a school, accepting that they only present a pupil view which needs to be put alongside staff and inspectors' views. They usually yield important information on issues which are difficult to assess otherwise, such as the pupil-reported level of bullying in the school, which is as important for the school to know as it is for any inspector to report. Many inspectorates will compare your survey results with the norms from many other comparable schools – effectively a standardised assessment, and using comparisons with norms to take into account the 'mischievous response rate' that have occurred in the norms as well as in your school.

Inspectors will assess pupil and personnel records, incident and other welfare records (such as records of fire drills, administration of medication, and records of complaints, accidents and punishments), together with practice documents. They are likely to pay particular attention to how any staff handbook or boarding practice document you use for reference on how to deal with boarding and welfare issues, measures up to the relevant standards. All schools should have key policies, such as a child protection policy on prevention of abuse and how staff (including junior and 'gap' staff) should respond to any suspicion or allegation, and a policy on countering bullying. Increasingly, inspectors are also interested in how the school carries out and records risk assessments to identify and counter significant health and safety hazards. In relation to policies and practice documents, what is important is what is actually used and followed in practice – and how what happens in the front line in the house matches up to the school's stated policy. As an example, most schools have a disciplinary policy, but sometimes there may be some punishments (often termed 'idiosyncratic punishments') which are not part of the approved policy – perhaps invented by an overzealous or inexperienced prefect or gap student, or brought in by a new member of staff.

The school should expect inspectors to act reasonably, and there are some conventions that inspectors should follow. They should observe common courtesies and the normal conventions of the school, should not inappropriately breach confidentiality of individuals, should not show prejudice against private education or the legitimate ethos of the school, should base their findings properly on evidence, and should not normally interview any pupil alone (unless there is a justifiable and exceptional reason). If the school considers that an inspector has behaved unrea-

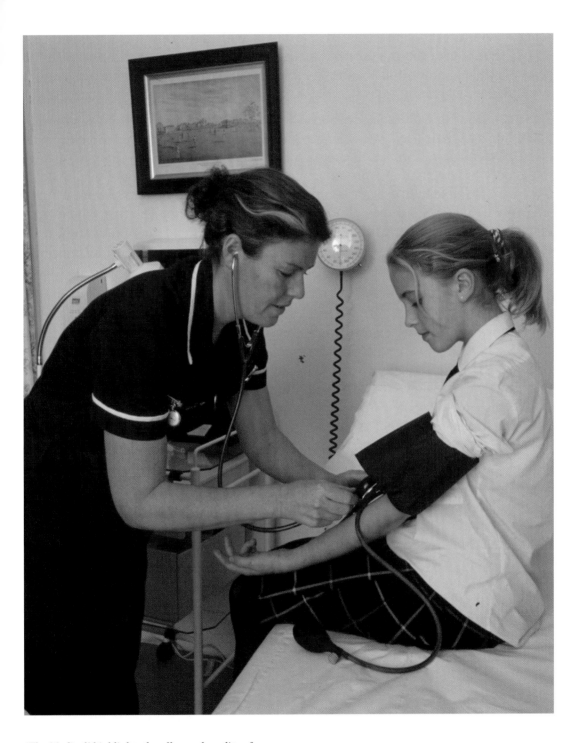

'The Medical' highlights the all-round quality of care.

sonably and the problem cannot be resolved with the inspector concerned, the school should take the matter up directly with the inspecting authority, with the head of the inspection unit or the Director of Social Services (under the current system), and if necessary through the authority's formal complaints procedure.

Reports following welfare inspections should give the inspectors' findings in relation to the standards used, with clear evidence for key findings, and with two kinds of recommendation. First are those recommendations considered necessary to fulfil the duty to safeguard and promote pupil welfare, which the school would clearly be wise to implement as soon as practicable, and secondly, more general welfare advice which the school may choose whether to implement. The first type of recommendation should include reference to the relevant standard, and the timescale for implementation. Most inspectors will send a draft report for factual checking and comment by the school before the report is finalised. If your house is involved in a welfare inspection, you should certainly ask to see a copy of the draft report so that you can feed your own comments into any response by the school.

Up to now, welfare inspections under the Children Act have come free of any charge, and welfare inspection reports have not been published, only going to the Head and Governors and relevant government departments. It is likely that in future, schools will have to pay fees to the inspecting body (in fact, other kinds of residential establishment always have done – such as elderly persons' homes, children's homes, and even playgroups and childminders), and welfare reports will be public documents, available to anyone on request. Again, welfare reports on many other kinds of establishment have always been published.

Schools will wish to know what can happen if the worst comes to the worst, and the inspectors consider that the school is failing in its legal duty to safeguard and promote boarders' welfare. The law is very clear on this. Inspectors carrying out welfare inspections under the Children Act have a legal duty to notify the Secretary of State (in practice, the office of the Registrar of Independent Schools) if they consider that the school has failed to safeguard and promote the welfare of any pupil it accommodates. Because this is a legal duty, it is not negotiable, and a notification has to be made unless the inspectors are satisfied that no failure has occurred. Inspectors should always inform the school if they intend to make a notification, and therefore it is appropriate to ask whether notification is intended after any inspection.

If a notification of failure to safeguard and promote welfare is made, it is important to know whether the inspectors are making any specific recommendation to the Registrar of Independent Schools. The inspectors themselves have no legal powers over the school, beyond inspecting it and reporting their findings, and cannot themselves take any enforcement action against you or the school. The Registrar however can, as the school is registered with the Secretary of State and relies on that registration to continue to operate as a school. If a notification of failure is made, the most likely next step, assuming that the failure is not extreme, is that an Official Letter will be sent by the Registrar's office asking for an undertaking on action to rectify matters, probably by implementing the recommendations of the welfare report. A follow up visit to the school is then likely. For a more serious failure, or a failure to rectify matters, a Notice of Complaint may be issued, requiring specific changes; if this ever happens at your school, it is essential that such a Notice is complied with, because continued failure to safeguard and promote welfare could otherwise jeopardise the school's registration – the Secretary of State can, subject to a Tribunal appeals process, cancel a school's registration and thus its licence to function as a school.

The best preparation for an inspection is to carry out a self-assessment against the standards to be used in the inspection, drawing up an action plan in response to any identified shortcomings. You should be able to obtain a copy of the inspection standards and criteria used by your own welfare inspectorate. To prepare for future inspections, or if there is no readily obtainable local document, schools can obtain the latest version of the National Boarding Standards. The process of self assessment might be to meet as a staff group (at all levels) to rate practice (honestly!) against each of the criteria listed, and to ask small groups of pupils to do the same (again, ask pupils at different levels, not only seniors or prefects). Then decide on what action to take where there are low ratings. It is important to pay particular attention to issues on which there are widely differing views, or a consistent discrepancy between staff and pupils, or between senior staff and junior colleagues. It is also worth re-reading any previous welfare report on the school or house, noting what has happened in response to any recommendation it contained.

It is worth carrying out two more specific exercises. One specialist area for self assessment, as a matter of school routine as well as to prepare for future inspection, is that of risk assessment. To carry out a basic risk assessment, consider systematically (involving pupil input) your premises and activities (including illicit as well as legitimate ones!), physically touring your premises, and separately running through your pupil activities. Identify hazards, rate the likelihood and seriousness of any injury or harm they may cause, any reasonable means of minimising or countering them, and the action necessary to reduce or manage the risks you have identified. Plan a process to implement and to monitor the implementation of your plan, and repeat the risk assessment at regular intervals (new risks have a habit of being discovered!). Pay particular attention to any 'near misses' where harm was narrowly avoided, asking colleagues and pupils to identify these. You cannot eliminate risk, and cannot run a school without risk, but the aim is to reduce forseeable and unnecessary risks.

The second specific exercise worth carrying out both as a part of school welfare monitoring routine and in preparation for any future inspection, is to self-check the school's staff recruitment checking procedures. All schools are required to carry out specific checks on all staff and other adults to whom they are going to give substantial opportunity for unsupervised access to pupils – and this is a common area of failure in the welfare duty. In a boarding setting, the adults to be checked are not only teachers, but the many adults in contact with pupils in boarding houses or in school activities – including ancillary staff, adult members of staff families living in houses, and gap students. It is well worth working with the Bursar (or whoever carries out staff checks) to draw a random sample of personnel files (including non-teaching staff and gap students) and initiate a simple search for a record of each of the checks specified in relevant welfare standards (such as the National Boarding Standards) having been carried out on recent appointments. If the result shows shortcomings, action needs to be taken before an inspector makes the same discovery.

The process of inspection can serve three very clear functions, separately from any question of possible, but rare, enforcement action: first to provide clear independent and external feedback to the school on its welfare practice, both positive and where necessary, negative; secondly to provide early warning and recommended corrective action on any failings or developing problems in welfare provision (try to regard inspection reports as one source of management consultancy to the school!); thirdly, through the publication of clear standards and criteria, to provide the school with guidance on accepted sound welfare practice.

No inspection process can ensure sound welfare practice – that is the school's duty. At best an inspection is like an MoT test for a vehicle: a systematic assessment by a welfare subject specialist of issues that may not otherwise be routinely checked, although limited to the standards specified and only fully valid on the day it was conducted. However, while the process of inspection is never popular, it can best be viewed not as something to be defended against, but rather like the outcome of that MoT test – or, to change the analogy, of a building survey – as producing information which either reassures, or which identifies matters that merit attention to restore reliable welfare.

Roger Morgan is the Chief Inspector, Oxfordshire County Council.

Chapter 14

Houseparenting in Perspective

by Charlie Bush

Headmaster, Eastbourne College

Tuesday 2 June 1992 – extract from the duty tutor's log

A busy day training House Prefects for next year at Elmore Abbey followed by a practical session in the evening so the lower sixth were not around. Charlie G was efficient on duty in House. Andrew W adding extra style by putting the folks to bed with guitar accompaniment. The Pied Piper of Blackheath. Prep was fine. The prospect of science exam on the morrow kept the Year 11 busy. Post Prize Day dollops of work taking effect elsewhere. Year 11 claim that revision is boring. How true! John H claims that sheer hunger makes it impossible to do prep – problem is that food causes hyperactivity. He learns about Catch 22: but doesn't understand it. He will, however, sometime. Deep discussion in basement dorm on Primitive Indo-European and Cyrillic script. Who was St Maeavior? Mike F reveals that his Dad is fluent in Tok Pisin, a New Guinea Creole. We certainly live and learn.

It is easy to make assumptions as to why one accepts a Head's invitation to teach in a boarding school. It may be that a post is accepted out of ignorance of the expectations of a 24 hour a day, seven day a week involvement; it may be, without a boarding background a post is accepted out of curiosity; or alternatively it may be that a lifetime of teaching was launched by a ten year stint away from home as a boarder during the formative years. Whatever the background there is soon the discovery that living within a boarding school provides a richness of opportunity for staff and pupils. There are immediate personal challenges to face. There is an expectation of extra-curricular commitment which competes for priority with academic preparation time and forces an aspiring teacher to become fully involved.

In common with many others, I have no doubt that during my first two years teaching at a boarding school, I learnt more about life than I contributed. The balance changes with time and experience. At the start the commitment was full and I was excited by the many competing enthusiasms in Common Room. New teachers often arrive with missionary zeal for some chosen area and their expertise launches the clay-pigeon society or the bridge club, or offers pupils the delights of gym, dance or wine tasting. There is also tutoring in a House and the responsibilities of a duty night. This is an area where the inexperienced are untrained. A new tutor, who has little background in the ways of a House, can be caught out on an early duty night by a precocious pupil set on mischief. Naivety can make the tutor easy prey for those with a sense of humour who try a practical joke during the informality of life after prep. Those educated in the system are better prepared.

Pupils have the advantage that they know the territory, often old and confusing buildings; they also know the routines. A tutor's duty is often to ensure that routines happen and in a well-run House these operate without the need for prefect or duty adult to intervene, as the House knows the times. Indeed an adult's lack of familiarity for the routines can be an advantage as most members of the House are not willing to try out an unknown adult. They meet bedtime deadlines without a murmur and the prefect appears at 11 pm to tell you that the House is in bed. As a new tutor you will take that announcement at face value, fully believing that this has been a wonderful duty night. You leave for home reassured by the calm of the House possibly after a debrief with the Houseparent, who no doubt will offer some liquid refreshment.

Whatever your background it is likely that a well-oiled House induction process will prepare you for some of the eventualities. After only a term a new tutor will probably feel more secure and in control. Familiarity for the tutor can make the job easier, or harder – that is a measure of character – but if it is to be done properly, there will be a dependence on 'walking the beat' along with the House mobile telephone, rather than sitting in the study marking.

Tutoring is essentially about talking to people. A successful tutor will use personality and social skills to develop a relationship, first by showing an interest in the tutee's life or family. A tutorial relationship that starts as a stilted and uneasy ten minute chat over 'how much I hate chemistry', can in a few years generate a lifetime friendship with the family and an invitation to attend an ex-tutee's wedding. It all depends on time – for good tutoring takes a lot of time – and with ten or so tutees, and lessons to teach, books to mark or sporting teams to coach there are many other demands. Sufficient one-to-one contacts are rarely possible for a teacher who has many other responsibilities. Time spent though is productive, for the building of a strong relationship could make all the difference for the tutee; it could divert the sort of stupidity for which adolescent children are renowned; it could offer the vital advice that changes a decision or direction, or it could just provide the still contact point in an otherwise turbulent world. The process of tutoring asks demanding questions of an inexperienced tutor who is often new to the boarding environment. It will soon become apparent that the boarding environment offers great scope for such tutoring.

Not all tutor/tutee relationships blossom into strength but the model is clear and the tutorial opportunity offers a chance to understand how a school works. There is the information written in the *Induction Booklet for new teachers* and there is what actually happens. The same is true in a House as is demonstrated by the difference in expectations by way of start of prep, social time or bedtime conflicting with what actually happens. In well run Houses and Schools these are not far apart but they are rarely exactly the same. The House involvement allows a new teacher to develop first an appreciation, and then an understanding for what is sometimes called the 'grey area' – that part of school life that lies between the established rules and what is standard practice. It is the ideal training ground for a future Houseparent as all the skills and understanding of a good tutor are much needed in leading a House as a Houseparent.

Teachers who do not learn about the 'grey area' are unlikely to make good Houseparents, for a House, like a home, does not run on rules in the same way that a battalion or battleship does. Rules must exist in a House but only as the basic framework. Fairness and firmness are essential if a House is to operate successfully but there must also be a genuine but subtle understanding that the reality of life is not a series of judgements between black and white. Some schools have tariff systems for smoking and drinking which moves a persistent offender inexorably towards the edge of the expulsion cliff. This system only works if compassion can be shown towards the worst offender.

Expulsions, which are often the inevitable result of such a tariff system, for such perennial indulgences of teenage life – the cigarette here or there, the surreptitious trip to the pub or the bottle in a bedsit – are wrong. Teenagers will make mistakes and continue to play the system but in a wider context it is understanding that must be sought, not the resort to regular punishment. The tariff system only works properly if occasional exceptions are made, as in every school there will be those for whom the best entreaties and endless patience do not bring improvement. Such children often come from confused family backgrounds, or have rebellious natures. The Houseparent's role must be to try to keep them on course to enable them to grow and develop within the school community. Nevertheless not all pupils will succeed, and there must also be a clear identification of when enough is enough. It will be the Head not the Houseparent who makes this judgement. A good Houseparent will publicly defend a charge to the last even when logic suggests there are few options left. It is always for a Head to administer the final option.

Once you live and tutor in a boarding environment it may naturally follow that you will want at some stage to spend time at the heart of the school as a Houseparent. If you like the boarding ethos, then you must spend time as a Houseparent living at the centre of the wheel for those in your House. All that you have done as tutor will have prepared you for the task. A new aspect in the Houseparenting role will be the greater need for liaison with parents. This often involves assisting with interpretations. A parent sometimes has to learn to understand the school; a child has to understand a parent or vice versa; a teacher's approach must be explained to a child; the school interpreted to a pupil. It is the thorough understanding of the school, gained from years as a tutor, that enables the Houseparent to second guess where communication is failing and needs to be addressed. There are however some parents who may never be reconciled and the last resort, usually after some painful meetings and telephone conversations, must be for the child to be withdrawn. The situation can be all the harder when the dealing is through guardians. A school cannot suit every child and every family – some relationships are just incompatible.

The rhythms of life in a boarding House are fundamental and unique. The difficult Saturday night experience has to be experienced to be understood. Appreciating the pressures that can persuade a misguided teenager to become blotto on vodka, steal from friends, bully, do mad things like climbing dangerously on top of buildings or even, in tragic circumstances, commit suicide, have to be understood from an insider's perspective. Such dreadful situations bring home the full realisation of the enormity of the responsibility. It is reassuring that schools now have excellent pastoral care networks, enhanced by a full understanding of the implications of the Children Act and the pervasive Social Service Inspections. These inspectors have learnt a lot too over the years.

When given the choice to become a Houseparent, the exhausting, invigorating, infuriating and wholly absorbing nature of the job should be highlighted. There is nothing better in education. I do recommend the advice given to a new Houseparent by a senior colleague:

> "If you trust them, they'll let you down,
>   if you don't trust them, they'll do you down;
>   it's better to be let down than done down"

And in almost every context this is still true. They certainly will let you down, for lying is in human nature, most evidently when pupils are trying to get out of something. There are the small white lies and the big whoppers and it is as well to spot the difference. Almost every child will lie at some stage to save their own skin. The unofficial code of conduct is not 'to tell on one's mates' and a lie in school life is considered a more honourable response than the truth, if the truth will implicate a friend. This is not a statement of low morality, it is merely deep-seated teenage loyalty. Similarly beware of unsolicited admissions of someone else's guilt for that is unusual.

Different schools have different cultures and it is generally in the larger communities where traditions of honesty are harder to instill. This is merely a function of the size of a school. In smaller schools where everyone is known, it is easier to encourage a basic expectation of honesty and harder for pupils to get away with things. Knowing when to press for truth and when to let a lie lie is a matter of experience for a Houseparent, but if a pupil is lying, one must never let them think they have got away with it. A basic statement that they are not believed, but that the matter is not going to be pursued, is a better response than appearing naïve or stupid. Such statements should always be made clearly and unambiguously to a pupil for they imply understanding of the 'going rate'. Parents often do not understand such adolescent mores and subsequent parental reaction to accusations of lying can be hard to defend. There are ways and means of saying the same thing, and occasionally the delicate euphemism may be right for parental ears but not for a pupil, and vice versa. This is where experience and advice help.

Sex and drugs are also tricky problems. A Head of House in my acquaintance always carried a condom in his wallet ("Sir, for emergencies in the holidays"). He was an excellent Head of House, loyal, shrewd, caring and wise but he was also a 'modern man', as he described himself. A tricky issue, for, as was agreed, there is only one use for such an item and were he to be found using it in school, he and another pupil would be expelled. Disciplining the Head of House, particularly a good one, is not an easy task. So much in that role depends on the building of a strong relationship of trust and understanding. Good communication and the empathy for shared objectives within a House are essential. Similar difficult discussions are needed with individuals who show the potential for sexual relationships. The sensitivities are all the greater if the pupils concerned have reached the age of consent or are potentially homosexual. Rewards will be great if an embarrassing and future-threatening event is avoided. This all requires oceans of time if it is to be done properly.

Just as Houseparents rarely have the time to give close attention to an individual on a regular basis over a long period, so individual help for, and training of, a Head of House does not always get done. When it does the spin-offs are considerable. So too with training House prefects and the most efficient system I have met for this was the Housemaster who used to get all his Upper Sixth Form pupils back a day early at the start of the September term. In 24 hours he inducted the lot, house prefects and others, discussed the issues affecting the House, set the 'targets' for the year, got everyone to complete their UCAS forms and ensured everything was absolutely in place for the arrival of new pupils and parents, the next day. There was also a formal dinner to start the year in style, to build team spirit and forge good relationships. There is no substitute for time spent and, in a busy term with so may other commitments, time is often not possible to find. Investing such time in pupil leadership is always desirable as it will mean that the House is more effectively run. Views differ on the desirability of keeping the same pupil as Head of House for the whole year. Consistency is good but such a policy reduces opportunity for others.

Drugs remain prevalent and schools now have a much more humane and understanding appreciation of the ready availability of soft drugs in our society than was once the case. No school tolerates those who push, use or import drugs. The message is spread through a PHSE programme, individual tutoring with suspect pupils and appropriate communication with home. Regular talks to year groups by such individuals as Phil Cooper, a reformed drug addict, who uses current press headlines to spread his message, have brought the problem into the open. It still offers a big challenge to the Houseparent who discovers drugs in any form, but it is less of a fear than it was, because schools generally have a clearly defined policy, and one telephone call to the Head or Deputy ensures full guidance and support for any action taken. The advance of science has helped and many schools use urine samples or swipe test suspected pupils. Of course the adult perspective on drugs is still different from a teenager's but that difference is changing. Teenagers understand the considerable consequences of involvement at school and do not want to get caught. Those that wish to experiment will always find a supply. The idea that pupils at school in a town are more likely to meet drugs than those in a country school is a myth. This was highlighted by the story of the boy who imported drugs to a school by purchasing his supply from his home village, a hamlet of ten houses. His supplier lived next door.

Nowhere is the difference in interpretation between the generations more evident than in the story of a boy expelled for possession of drugs ten years ago. After the full investigation, the visit to the Head, the arrival of the parents, matron's assis-

A House Group Meeting addresses wider school issues and irons out problems.

tance in packing the trunk and collecting of possessions. The sad farewells, the apologies from pupil to Houseparent and apologies from Houseparent to parents – for parents put their child in a Houseparent's care and do not expect it to end in such failure, whatever the potential for disaster in their child. After these formalities came the final farewell. As the Housemaster was trying to find words for the emotional moment, he wished the boy a successful life, free from troubles and similar involvement, and in the presence of a weeping mother and tearful father, the boy replied "Good bye Sir, please can I have my water pistol back that you confiscated last week!"

It is the business of the Houseparent to run his or her House. Deep down the pupils must know that a Houseparent cares. If the environment is warm, the atmosphere friendly and the discipline firm but fair, the House will succeed. Successful and happy pupils generally bring contented parents. There is more to it, but at the core, this is the task. If the atmosphere is right, with regular adult contact of the right kind, the House will thrive. Good recruitment will follow and the good reputation of the House will enhance the career of the Houseparent. No-one should move into a senior management position in a boarding school, with the exception of the Director of Studies, without the experience of being a Houseparent. In one sense they would miss doing the 'best job in teaching' and in another they will have less understanding of the school from the pupil's perspective. There are celebrated successful exceptions to this rule which goes to prove that it is there to be broken, but as a generalisation it seems good. The test of patience, temper, administrative skills, stamina, resilience, integrity and character needed to succeed as a Houseparent will provide evidence that he or she is ready for sterner challenges.

Heads who have not been Houseparents have to watch carefully that they understand life from the House perspective and appreciate the relentless pressure in say the ninth week of term. A Head can do a very effective job without 'Houseparenting' experience but he or she will only have been fully tested by actually running a House. There is a high regard in HMC schools for Houseparents and in our league table world there is a concern about the status of Heads of Departments. There are different stresses on holders of the two posts, the HoD's work is generally strategic, and the Houseparent's ongoing, frenetic and persistent. Different people are suited to different roles and can have completely different views of the same school as a result. Harmony is important to avoid friction that one side or the other should have greater status or enjoy a greater allowance. Those who have done both jobs well and have a sense of management reality will be very well prepared for Headship.

As a consequence of living in the world of 'Child Protection' a Houseparent must be alert for legal issues which have the potential to develop unpredictably. In schools where pastoral meetings are frequent there will be enough signals for a new Houseparent to call for help. Knowing who is the Child Protection Officer is only part of the business that includes regular contact with the line manager, usually a Deputy Head with pastoral responsibilities. This communication brings about the natural support and cover for any eventuality. No-one should feel alone in dealing with a crisis. If concerned, inform the Head, through the Deputy if necessary, as the Head will want to know when trouble is brewing. The Head who can input to a child through his or her personal contact, is rare. It is easier in small schools or when a Head makes this a priority. Not all Heads see it this way and nor can this be expected.

An interesting aside on Heads' decisions, is the occasion where a pastoral or disciplinary decision is made by the Head involving a pupil or a member of staff. Such decisions do not always meet universal agreement from pupils or staff, and even Houseparents can sometimes work up a head of steam over the consequences or implications. It can be also true that none of them actually knows the full facts. On some matters the full facts may only ever be known by the Head and thus a decision can only really be made or understood by the Head. This is not intended to be a diatribe on the infallibility of Heads' judgement, but there are areas in a busy, closely networked boarding community when wires get crossed and frustration results. Those who criticise often do not, and may never, know all the facts. The 50-something year old in Common Room may be less committed to the job than he or she used to be, but what they often do have is a wider perspective which comes from the wisdom of age. It is rare for retired Houseparents to criticise the current generation as they know how hard the job was and how much harder it has become. They also know how complicated the picture is. Infiltrating some of this perception throughout Common Rooms can make for happier staff rooms.

There are many challenges for the future of boarding. The universal one is that of numbers and the right balance of international and home based pupils. The day boarding mix is increasingly important and schools vary on whether the desirable structure is for day pupils in a boarding House, boarders in a day House or separate entities. Different schools come up with different solutions which will become more diverse if times get harder. Individual schools generate their own particular styles. There is too much provision for boarding and in time the pressure on schools will mount. Good boarding schools abound but the town verses country debate, the single-sexed verses co-educational arguments, will continue. Views differ on the value of big ISIS exhibitions for selling schools and they may well be seen as a phenomenon of the nineties. The international exhibitions overseas are popular and different.

The challenges of the 16-19 changes will impact on boarding too. Boarding schools have traditionally sucked up pupils' spare time effectively with a rich and diverse extra-curricular programme. This was founded on a relatively free Lower Sixth year with no exams and great opportunities. Some of this extra-curricular enrichment is under threat; so too is the assumption that senior pupils should in their final terms serve the community and give something back to it. Such expectation of service from seniors has been central to school life. It will be interesting to see the impact of greater pressure after September 2000 with three external exam years in succession, modules twice a year, extra time pressures of four or more subjects in the lower sixth form, without the availability of study time of old. Some schools have taken on the International Baccalaureate as a way to seek breadth but the implications of a greater academic commitment seem to imply less opportunity for extra-curricular activities. This is a challenge facing the boarding schools, whose lifeblood has been based on the extra-curricular enhancement and full rounding of people, complementing the academic picture.

This full commitment mirrors Francis Drake's approach in his famous speech "to complete the game of bowls and beat the Spaniards too". Now the 'bowls' is under pressure and the Spanish is added alongside three science subjects to absorb what might have been perceived as free time. Resolving the academic and extra curriculum challenges is for the senior managers. If they get it wrong, pupils will suffer and the Houseparents will have to manage the situation. There is no alternative but to embrace change and move forward, but in the boarding environment we must do all we can to maintain the quality of what is offered.

An old-fashioned remedy suggests that all will be well if the House can be put to bed at the appointed hour for pupils to get enough sleep; but they are young and for many the late night experiences of coffee, chats with tutor and others, makes boarding so special and so enriching. Each generation has its challenges and perhaps those today pale into insignificance with the revolution of the late sixties. Boarding school children are now living in a far better disciplined and purposeful environment than was once the case. That is a measure of progress and highlights the expectation of future change. The ICT revolution will soon make a huge impact on House management, security, learning and entertainment. These challenges are just starting and the schools that find the effective solutions will do well.

29 February 1992 - extract from duty tutor's log

Just another Saturday Night? Brisk business at early check-in; some encouraging hockey results; some very tired boys. Year 10 Dance seems quite popular; House Bar attracts Lower Sixth custom. Year 9 go in search of girls - they try two Houses and still return early. Area outside House quite crowded later in the evening: girls keen to propose? Bedtime quite uneventful until the late arrival of three trusty(?) House Prefects. All three had consumed too much alcohol, but only one was in fighting mood.

"I'm 18 so I can do what I like!"

I wonder why he didn't say: "I'm 18 so I know I have responsibilities"?

Charlie Bush was a boarder at prep school. He was Housemaster of B1 House, Marlborough College from 1988-1993 when he became Headmaster of Eastbourne College. He was Director of the HMC Training Course for new Boarding Houseparents from 1996 - 1999.